MILITARY ETHICS

Nicholas G. Fotion is a professor of philosophy at Emory University where he teaches military ethics, medical ethics, ethical theory, and the philosophy of language. His publications, both in book and article form, cover all these fields. Most recently he coedited *Hare and Critics: Essays on Moral Thinking* and coauthored *Military Ethics: Guidelines for Peace and War*.

MILITARY
· ETHICS ·

Looking Toward the Future

Nicholas G. Fotion

HOOVER INSTITUTION PRESS • STANFORD UNIVERSITY • STANFORD, CALIFORNIA

Hoover Press Publication 397
Copyright © 1990 by the Board of Trustees of the
    Leland Stanford Junior University

First printing, 1990
96   95   94   93   92   91   90   9   8   7   6   5   4   3   2   1
Simultaneous first paperback printing, 1990
96   95   94   93   92   91   90   9   8   7   6   5   4   3   2   1

Manufactured in the United States of America
Printed on acid-free paper

Library of Congress Cataloging-in-Publication Data
Fotion, N.
    Military ethics : looking toward the future / Nicholas G. Fotion.
          p.   cm. — (Hoover Institution publication : 397)
    Includes bibliographical references and index.
    ISBN 0-8179-8971-4. — ISBN 0-8179-8972-2 (pbk.)
    1. Military ethics.   2. Munitions—Moral and ethical aspects.
I. Title.
U22.F64   1990   90-20447
174'.9355—dc20   CIP

Contents

· CHAPTER ONE ·

Pacifism and Realism Revisited

Introduction

To many people, talk about military ethics has the flavor of a joke—to some, even a sick joke—because it seems strange or contradictory to conjoin ethics with military matters. "Where on the battlefield can ethics be found," some ask, "when what goes on there represents a denial of the central ethical principles concerned with not killing, not committing violent acts, telling the truth, and respecting property?" To those in particular who sense the sickness of the joke, what bothers is that conjoining "military," "war," "warrior," and "weapon" to "ethics" and "morality" gives the former group of concepts a sense of respect they do not deserve. One consequence of this conjoining is that the subjects of military and war ethics are placed on a pedestal along with such legitimate subjects of study as medical, environmental, legal, and family ethics. Another result is that those who engage in war can now have their consciences soothed by supposing that they are fighting ethical wars. Worse still, they can actually come to be proud of the work they do—work concerned, after all, with destroying people, property, and the environment.

These reactions to ethics in war have existed since ancient times (Lao Tzu 1972, 65; Shang Yang 1972, 138–39). But they are not always expressed linguistically with one voice. Some say that ethics and war are incompatible because they are contradictory concepts. Indeed, those who say this, the so-called realists, need not agree among themselves on why a contradiction exists here. Those who can be called contract realists think of war as excluding ethics because war represents a cancellation, for whatever reason, of those (ethical) contracts and practices in effect during peacetime (Sherman 1892, 119–20). Other realists, who can be called self-interest realists, argue that nations do not have ethical relations with one another even during peacetime, let alone during war (Shang Yang 1972, 138–39; Hobbes [1651] 1968, 266, part 2, chapter 21; Treitschke 1963, 53). However they arrive at their views, realists would agree that during war "anything goes." No ethical rules, principles, guidelines, or virtues restrain them on how they fight in war, and possibly even on when they should engage in war. Realists might, in fact, exhibit some restraint in war, but if they did, they would do so only for nonethical reasons. If it profited them in battle to take prisoners and then later treat them with respect, they might do so; otherwise, not.

Pacifists have quite different reasons for supposing that the concepts of ethics, on the one side, and military and war, on the other, cannot be conjoined. Like the realists, pacifists disagree among themselves about why their position is correct. However, they all agree that the realists are wrong in calling wars nonmoral. Wars are, instead, immoral. For the pacifists, wars are not times when ethics has no application. Rather, wars represent times when ethics can and should be applied, but is not. For them, to call certain wars moral or ethical is not so much a contradiction as a tragically mistaken ethical judgment.

How do pacifists disagree among themselves about why their position is correct? Some say that wars are immoral because they are commanded by religious authority not to engage in violence against human beings. Others deduce their pacifism from a principle of love or benevolence. Still others, for whatever reason, believe that human life is infinitely valuable and, therefore, no one is permitted to destroy it. Finally, other pacifists invoke certain basic duties or rights to explain their position, appealing to moral intuitions that inform them directly or indirectly about the wrongness of war.

It is not my purpose to attack or defend any of these explanations of the pacifist position except in passing. They have been grouped together to be ignored together. What they share to deserve such treatment is simply that they tend to be nonempirical. They present the pacifist position not as if it has jurisdiction based primarily on our experiences with war, but in terms of abstract appeals or principles. In and of itself, I have no quarrel with such an approach. It may be that pacifism can be made to work by appealing exclusively or primarily to abstract religious, philosophic, or ethical principles. So the reason these explanations are being ignored has nothing to do with their eventual credibility. They are being ignored in order to focus on other pacifist arguments.

Why do these other arguments deserve special attention? Unlike more abstract arguments that have whatever force they have always had, the arguments I will focus on seem to have more impact today than before. Because these arguments are partly based on our experiences with war (that is, being partly empirical), their force can increase or decrease with changes in the realities of war. In fact, the pacifist position can be presented as suggesting that modern wars are immoral where older wars were not necessarily so, or that modern wars are even more immoral than older ones. Because modern wars may have increased the force of certain versions of the pacifist position, this position needs to be revisited.

A similar revisiting is in order for the realist position. Like the pacifist position, certain versions have been left untouched by changes taking place in modern war and military practices. These versions will be ignored in this work except, again, in passing. Only those versions of realism seemingly strengthened (or weakened) by our current experiences with war will be discussed extensively.

In the end, revisiting both pacifism and realism will necessitate revisiting just-war theory. Such a theory, like pacifism and realism, does not represent one position. Especially when it comes to saying why their theory is correct, just-war theorists are prone to express the same disagreement among themselves as pacifists and realists. Nonetheless, by definition, these theorists agree that some wars are just while others are not. Holding a position between the pacifists and realists, they face the trick of determining which wars are just and which are not.

Revisiting Pacifism

Pacifists have always looked to actual wars, not abstract arguments, to defend their position. They have done so not just in essays but also in novels, written stories, poems, motion pictures, plays, art, and other forms of expression (Mayer 1966; Ryan 1983, 508–24). Thus, appealing to the horrible experiences of war in defense of pacifism is nothing new (Lao Tzu 1972, 64–66). It is also nothing new for these pacifists to make the judgment that the wars they write about are somehow worse than the ones others have written about in the past. What is new is that things seem to be worsening at an accelerating pace. Future wars, they claim, are not just going to be hellish, like all war in the past, but hellish in ways literally beyond our imagination (Westling 1984, 114–24).

What is bothersome to those not sympathetic with the pacifist position is that these judgments are based on facts, not just on some pacifist ideology. One does not have to be a genius to see that what fuels the judgments about the almost unimaginable hellishness of future wars is modern technology. Technology has put weapons into the hands of warriors so they can shoot faster and farther, do more damage, fight both day and night, and fight both under favorable and unfavorable weather conditions. Technology has given warriors other weapons as well. Many of them will be described in chapter 2. For now, it is enough to note that these increased capabilities may be reaching the point where modern military technology will soon be able to destroy whole societies not just with nuclear weapons, but with a variety of so-called conventional weapons.

This more empirical version of the pacifist position is not restricted to emphasizing just the inherent destructive potential of modern weapons. It is not only that once the war starts a new kind of hell with break loose, but that modern weapons actually increase the chances of war breaking loose. Modern weapons do this in two ways.

The first is related to the ability these weapons give military forces to strike quickly. Whereas in the past, military forces might take weeks or even months to strike the enemy, today they can do so at a moment's notice. This is especially true when you consider nuclear weapons mounted on ballistic missiles. But this point also has application with conventional weaponry. Missiles and rockets armed with nonnuclear weapons can strike just as quickly, and with devastating effect. Aircraft with speed and stealth technology can prostrate a nation within hours and thereby make it vulnerable to further attack. In addition, ground armies are far more mobile today than they were even in World War II because they can strike with mobilized artillery, infantry, and other quick-strike forces as well as with tanks. All this ability to strike quickly takes away the response time of nations intent upon pursuing peace. They cannot help but be more nervous about being attacked and be tempted, in turn, to react by building up their own military forces.

If potential enemies can strike quickly, response time to such strikes must also be quick. In the paranoid world of international politics it does not take much imagination to predict what happens next. Other nations, whether they view themselves as potential aggressors or not, will themselves become nervous, and this nervousness will translate into new weapons development and deployment to react against the original reaction. Then there will be a reaction to that reaction. Each side's military spokespersons will point to the weaknesses on "our" side and the vast strengths of the "other" side (Gervasi 1987, v–vi; Sivard, 1987:9). More of everything will be demanded to protect the fatherland or motherland. However, technology being what it is, each reaction will yield only momentary security. In the long run, the drive to protect oneself will lead to a gradual loss of security because the threat of potential attacks will force nations to build more destructive weapons with even quicker response-time features (Barnaby 1984b, 56–71). According to the pacifist argument we are developing, it will also lead to the increased possibility of a war breaking out. Given the fact that response times will be so short, accidents and misunderstandings will more likely lead to automatic aggressive or defensive military responses. These same response times will also make it difficult to stop a war once it has begun.

The second way modern military technology encourages war is more institutional. As we have just seen, response times to potential wars will be short. This has the additional consequence that military forces will be invited to "come as you are" to wars. Because the results of modern wars can be decided in minutes, hours, or days, these forces will necessarily do their fighting with whatever training they have been given before the war and with whatever weapons they have in hand. More than in the past, therefore, large military forces will need to be in place for whatever might happen. It is true that these standing forces might not be looking for a fight, so their mere presence will not always cause war. Still, according to the pacifist argument, standing military forces cannot help but be strongly tempted to look for tensions between nations and in some cases create tensions if only in their own minds. Beyond that, the military will be tempted to create actual tensions and perhaps even create wars. Insofar as they will be reacting in these ways, they will unavoidably be expressing a conflict of loyalty between serving the society by protecting it and serving their own interests. A war here and there might remind everyone just how much the military is needed. Having a standing military force always ready to protect you, it now appears, might not be so good for your health after all.

Nor is a standing military force good for one's pocketbook. It is an expensive institution to build and sustain, largely because it must be equipped with sophisticated and complicated weapons. This equipment, the pacifist will be quick to remind us, requires that still another institution be in place. If modern weapons could be designed, produced, and deployed quickly, it would be another story. But just as response time to war itself has lessened, the response time related to making weapons has increased. Weapon systems take years to design, manufacture, and put on line for use in war. To deal with possible future wars, therefore, it has become necessary to maintain a permanent and strong industrial base keyed to conceiving and producing these weapons. This means that the problems mentioned above associated with having a standing military force are duplicated with industry. Because this institution is a permanent one made up of various industries, its desire to serve society's needs and its own needs will not always coincide. Inevitably, in its search for profits and power, industry will do what it can to sell weapon systems to the military even if they are not needed. In addition, as with the military, it will often be in the interests of industry to have political tensions throughout the world maintained, if not to the boiling point, at least almost to that level. Once again, an institution ostensibly created to protect a society, but possessing its own special interests, will find it almost impossible to work in ways that do not put that society in jeopardy.

But there is more to the story. It is not as if there are two completely separate institutions working, consciously or unconsciously, in ways that sometimes jeopardize the welfare of those they are serving. Rather, both institutions are working together to form what has been popularly called a military-industrial complex. Actually, as many realize, it is more appropriately called a military-industrial-political complex (or even the Iron Triangle) because all three institutions strongly influence each other. The direction and strength of these influences differ, depending on the society. One way these influences manifest themselves in capitalistic societies is through financial contributions to key political figures (Smith 1988, 173–79). Another way is via contracts. If a major military contract to build an aircraft carrier means thousands of jobs in an area represented by several politicians, the temptation for those politicians to support that weapon system will be great. Both the military and industry will be delighted with that support, but so will labor and management in that district. So now the complex has become a military-industrial-political-labor complex. In contrast, in noncapitalistic or militaristic societies, the complex manifests itself with the military being represented directly in various political and other power circles.

However it happens, the complex will have benefits for all its members. Here is an example. The military might be interested in purchasing an expensive new fighter plane. It can afford to buy only 100 such planes during its next fiscal year. Industry will, no doubt, be happy to sell these planes. Still, if the price were lower, the military might buy 120. How can this be arranged? Quite simply by achieving economies of scale (Barnaby 1984e, 148–58). If the military, industry, and the politicians work as a team to sell 100 such planes overseas (and here we see the advantage of keeping the waters just below the boiling point or at times allowing things to actually boil over), industry can produce each plane more cheaply. A 10 percent or 20 percent discount might give the air force just the number of planes it had always wanted but could not afford before. Labor is happy because jobs will last longer from the increased amount of work. Also happy, of course, are the politicians, the company executives, and its stockholders.

Here is another example. This cozy arrangement involves industry offering jobs to military personnel who are a year or two from retirement. In return, industry receives special considerations in the form of less-than-scrupulous inspections of equipment delivered to the military (Lucas 1988, 1360–61).

One other aspect of this overall pacifist argument needs to be addressed: the opportunity costs of possessing standing military and industrial forces. Keeping these forces in place not only costs money as such but it takes away the opportunity we might have to use that money more productively. Military expenditures, it can be argued, do not benefit so many people as would expenditures directly aimed at improving such aspects of society as education, health care, the environment, housing, or transportation (Dumas 1984, 125–47). In this sense military expenditures can be viewed as a waste, a taking away of money that could be spent on more humanitarian concerns.

In a variety of ways, what this overall pacifist argument, the big argument, as I will call it, comes down to is that modern military technology makes war far more costly than in the past. As noted at the outset, pacifists can present other versions of their position that in no way are affected by the big argument. If, as one version would have it, killing one individual is infinitely wrong, any war that results in the death of one person is immoral. By the logic of infinity, a much more serious modern war is no more immoral than a small one because it too is (only) infinitely wrong. This argument or position is an example of what can be called unqualified (full-bodied or absolute) pacifism (Fotion and Elfstrom 1986, 3, 7–10, 32–36). It declares all wars to be immoral—without qualification. Because under this banner are found not only pacifists who believe in the infinity argument but also others who arrive there by other arguments, unqualified pacifism should not be viewed as a specific position but as covering many.

Some unqualified pacifists might be impressed by the big argument, but it it not likely. One reason they would not is that this argument conceivably makes some wars permissible. If what makes wars immoral is modern technology, it just might be possible that a simple nontechnological war someplace in human history could be counted as just. If so, unqualified pacifists would look for another argument to guarantee that even small old-fashioned wars are immoral. At best, these pacifists would treat the big argument as supplementing a more basic one. They might use the big argument to reassure any of their faltering followers who have lost sight of the impact of more basic pacifist arguments. Or the argument might be used as a conversion tool.

Who might be converted? Probably not their cousins the qualified pacifists. Very likely, these pacifists already believe in the big argument, in part, because they are partial toward experience-based arguments. Qualified pacifists generally oppose violence, and their opposition is stronger than it is with most people. But they still will allow for some exceptions. Whether these exceptions are found on the personal level, as when they will use violence to protect themselves, or on the larger social scene, as when they will allow for a rare just war, will vary with the individuals. Whatever the case, for these qualified pacifists there have been only a few ethical (just) wars. As to the future, given the big argument, or any variations of it, there cannot help but be even fewer just wars.

So if the big argument is a conversion tool, it will be used both by unqualified pacifists, as a supplemental argument, and their qualified relatives, probably as their main argument, to convert nonbelievers. Used as such, it appears to be a powerful argument, particularly because it is based in large part on almost undisputable factual claims. Whether nonbelievers should be converted is one of the two major questions to be answered in this study. The other is: Given the nature of modern war, should people be converted to realism? More on that question shortly. But with respect to the former question, more now needs to be said about the big argument (and later in chapter 2 about some modern weapons) before we can assess in later chapters this argument's potential to convert people to pacifism.

Most important, what needs saying is that the big argument is not really a single argument. It is convenient to talk of it as such, because all its parts speak to the direct and indirect high negative effects, or costs, of modern weaponry. Still, the argument can be broken down into four basic parts, or subarguments: the destructiveness of modern weapons, probably the main part of the big argument; the monetary and social costs of maintaining a military establishment, including this establishment's tendency to trigger war; the monetary and social costs of maintaining an industrial establishment, including the tendency this establishment has to trigger wars as well; and the opportunity costs of war and the constant vigilance needed to prevent it. Thus the big argument is well named because it is composed of several subarguments and because it is so influential when the ethics of modern war is being discussed.

About these subarguments it is important to make the following points. First, each is consequentialist in nature, or at least this is one plausible way it can be interpreted. When so interpreted, each argument essentially says that modern weapons bring about had results. The point can be made stronger. It is not just that these weapons yield bad consequences, but that having or using them leads to the worst possible consequences overall.

Second, when the big argument is interpreted in consequentialist terms, its users need to make assessments as to what counts as good and bad consequences. For pacifist purposes, this is not difficult to do. Bad consequences have to do with increased human (and perhaps nonhuman) suffering, and good consequences with minimizing such suffering as well as maximizing human happiness. The claim each part of the big argument makes, and therefore the claim inherent in the big argument as a whole, is that possessing and using modern weapons maximizes suffering and minimizes happiness.

Third, no subargument explicitly addresses the traditional distinction found in just-war theory between justice of the war (*jus ad bellum*) and justice in the war (*jus in bello*) equally. This distinction allows just-war theorists to separate the rightness or justice of a nation's involvement in a war from the rightness or justice of how the war is fought. It thus becomes possible for them to say of a nation at war that it might be fighting a just war justly, an unjust war justly, a just war unjustly, or an unjust war unjustly. Just-war theorists are interested in all these possibilities equally. In contrast, the distinction between the justice *of* and the justice *in* the war is of interest to unqualified pacifists only with respect to the fourth possibility because they view all wars as immoral. Thus there is no way for anybody to fight any war in a just manner. Still, it should be clear that the first part of the big argument focuses on *jus in bello* by pointing to the details of the injustice found in the slaughters that take place while wars are in progress; the other parts focus on the causes that tend to trigger modern wars in the first place. Again, for pacifists in general, there are no, or at best very few, good reasons for starting wars. But the reasons for starting wars mentioned in the big argument are especially bad because they appeal to selfishness. The military and industry act in ways that satisfy their own selfish institutional needs, even though others will suffer as a result.

Before putting this discussion of the big argument aside for now, three disclaimers are in order. For my purposes, it is not important that probably no one person or group is committed to the correctness of all parts of the big argument. It is enough that we often hear appeals to large portions of the argument when people lament about the possibility of future wars (Holmes 1989, 3; Sivard 1987, 9). I am interested more in the argument itself rather than in who holds it. And my intent is to make the big argument as strong as possible to see what force it has. In this same spirit, it is also not important to attempt to state a final version of this argument in this chapter. Rather, as it has been characterized so far, it should be thought of as a first approximation of an argument that will be made stronger by deletions or additions suggested by further discussion. Finally, I am not claiming that anyone who believes any single part, or possibly two parts, of the big argument is a pacifist of some stripe or other. It is certainly conceivable that some admirer of war and conflict would agree that the military has a tendency to cause war, and be happy for all that. It is also conceivable that others might go part way with the big argument by admitting, for example, that the military-industrial complex is dangerous in many ways, and still not go so far as to condemn this complex. What I am claiming, however, is that the package of parts, or subarguments, that forms the big argument is well fitted together, and that holding onto most of these parts constitutes being a certain kind of pacifist.

Revisiting Realism

If the introduction of modern weaponry has allowed pacifism to be strengthened by the big argument, it would seem to follow that realism must be weakened. Paradoxically this is not so. As has been suggested already, some forms of realism are not affected in any way by modern weapons development. Contractual realism is certainly not, because, for this position both old-fashioned and modern wars represent cancellations of contracts and practices that encouraged nations to be civil to one another during peacetime. Nor, as has been noted, is self-interest realism affected, because on this theory nations never act on the moral level with respect to one another anyway—neither in peace nor war. Yet one version of realism is affected. It can be called inability realism. In part, this version is animated by a philosophical or logical point about what we (moderns at least) understand ethics to be. That point is often expressed as " 'ought' implies 'can.' " That is, we cannot obligate people or nations to do those things they do not have the ability to do. It makes no sense to say to Sam that he ought to jump over the (mile-wide) lake. Nor to obligate him to lift a main battle tank with his bare hands. Nor even to tell him to change his emotions on a moment's notice, as if all he had to do is turn a switch off or on. This is the philosophical leg of the inability realist position. As these examples show, this leg can be used to support arguments both in military and nonmilitary matters.

The second leg of inability realism is more empirical and supports the realist claim that there are things we can do during peacetime we cannot consistently do during war. During peace, when we are surrounded by people in the habit of living ethical lives, when we have societal pressures to maintain these ethical (and legal) habits, and when things are generally calm, we can be told in a meaningful way not to kill, steal, or lie. Such telling is meaningful because we have the ability to do these things. The conditions of peace themselves make it possible for us to choose right or wrong. But during war, things are different. Most of the social fabric that helps us contain our behavior within certain bounds is torn away. It is true that as soldiers we are still told not to kill people on our own side. Presumably we have control of our behavior to that extent. But when it comes to the enemy, control is not possible. No one can expect us, as soldiers, to behave consistently like boy scouts when violence is raging all around us, when we have been taught to kill the enemy, and when, as is often the case, the enemy commits atrocious acts. Under conditions of war, all of us, soldier and civilian alike, lose all sense of control over our behavior. We inevitably become more like beasts than humans, at least insofar as the enemy is concerned.

It is interesting to note that pacifists might agree with this overall assessment of what actually happens during war. For them, that is all the more reason why we should not engage in war. For the inability realists, in contrast, our inability to guide our behavior by ethical norms during war only shows, or helps to show, that ethics simply has no place in war.

But how is this version of realism helped by modern weapons development? Like the pacifists, the realists are all too happy to argue that modern wars make it even more difficult to control human behavior. As bad as it was before, modern wars make it even more difficult for both the warriors and their leaders to even think about the ethics of taking prisoners, harming civilians, and using only "ethical" weapons. All that can be expected of these people is that they get their job done as quickly and efficiently as possible.

The parallel with the pacifist argument here has more than passing interest. Both sides can agree that modern wars are worse than the older variety. Both sides can also agree that wars in general, but modern wars in particular, are dehumanizing. Both sides can even agree that wars make it impossible for those who participate in them to carry out their moral duties when it comes to dealing with the enemy. These areas of agreement, thus far, focus on justice in the war. Where they disagree is that the pacifists will go on to say that because war is full of injustice, we must avoid it. The realists' reply is that because those in war can act neither justly nor unjustly, we must avoid ethics.

The parallel between the two positions extends to issues concerned with the justice of the war. Like pacifists, realists can argue that modern weaponry has changed things so that this weaponry's quick-response features and the need for standing military institutions and for military-oriented industrial organizations also make controlling human behavior, to the level demanded by ethics, quite impossible. Still, during peace-time it certainly is still possible to think in terms of our self-interest or, as it might be better put, our survival. Thinking that way is instinctive. Yet when the pressures of survival are severe, it is quite out of the question to expect people to behave ethically. Of course, pacifists would say that it is exactly under such pressures when an appeal to ethical principles is most important. But realists would reply that such appeals are meaningless when it is not in our power to do anything about them. For the realists, it makes no difference whether we have lost this power during the stress of war or as the result of the threats we face during peacetime.

Just-War Theory

Just-war theorists would also have a reply: in spite of the emotions of war, some choices are possible so that ethics still has a place in war, even in modern war. To the pacifists, these theorists would argue against any radical new way of looking at the ethics of wars just because of modern weapons. In later chapters we will look in detail at the validity of these two replies and at any counter replies that might come from the realists and pacifists. The goal in this chapter is not to assess the arguments pro and con, but to get preliminary statements of them down on paper. In this spirit, several things should be said about the just-war theory position to give a sense of balance to the presentation of the major theories.

I have spoken of just-war theory as a middle position between the extremes. In a way, this is misleading because only the pacifist position is on an ethical dimension with just-war theory. The realists, it will be recalled, cannot be found on this dimension. They have fallen off the end, as it were, because they believe that wars have nothing to do with ethics. For just-war theorists to be literally in the middle on one (ethical) dimension, we would have to invent an ethical position that says all or practically all wars are morally just, and that in fighting such wars morality permits warriors to do whatever they wish. I suppose such a position could be or has been invented. Someone could argue that wars reward those who are most fit to survive, and that it is good that the most fit survive. Still, because this is not considered a live option in current discussions of military ethics, I will not discuss it at all. Whether it deserves such neglect or not, it is equivalent to some versions of the classic (nonethical) realist position—in practice if not in theory. Both would permit a nation to fight wars when they please, and as they please.

If, then, we focus not on the theory (that is, whether a theory is or is not found in the ethical realm) but on whether and how wars are fought, it still makes sense to say that just-war theory falls in the middle. Thus, for whatever (ethical) reasons they give, unqualified pacifists condemn all wars at one extreme; and realists, for whatever reasons they give, condemn no wars. Again, realists might appeal to prudence to advise against starting a war or against fighting a war in a certain way, but they would countenance no ethical praise or criticism.

Yet even if it makes sense to say that just-war theorists are standing in the middle, this does not mean they are all standing together at one point. Even less does it mean that they are standing in the middle for the same reasons. Some just-war theorists might be utilitarians (Fotion and Elfstrom, 1986), others rights theorists (Walzer 1977), and still others might stand there by appealing to tradition (Johnson 1984). But as it is being discussed at the moment, standing or not standing in the same place in the middle has nothing to do with these reasons why. Instead, it deals with where just-war theorists stand with respect to the extremes of unqualified pacifism and all forms of realism. And it should be clear that some of them lean in the direction of the pacifists while others lean in the opposite direction. So although just-war theorists are in the middle, in the sense of holding a position between two extremes, some may be hard to distinguish from those who hold seemingly extreme positions. Are just-war theorists who condemn 95 percent of all past wars really still in that tradition, or are they better labeled weak-kneed pacifists?

For this study, it is important not to forget questions like this. If, as I am arguing, labels such as pacifism and just-war theory encourage us to forget that the discussion is over a matter of degrees on a dimension, we will misunderstand the discussion. In this sense, the originally posed question—"Should the big argument convince us that the pacifist position is correct?''—is misleading. We should be asking instead, ''Insofar as it might be correct, does the big argument force us either to become pacifists or to move in that general direction?''

One final point in this preliminary presentation of just-war theory needs to be made. It should not be thought that this theory is completely on the defensive, as the result of the changes taking place in how wars are and soon will be fought. Just-war theorists can argue that the big argument and the arguments of the inability realists do not represent all the facts of modern war. That is, they can argue that the ''extremists'' on both sides select only those facts that suit their arguments. So they can reply by way of alleging that their own more complete picture of how modern wars can be fought allows for ethics to have a place in modern wars, just as it had a place in the wars of the past. Just-war theorists can also argue that even the facts cited by their extremist opponents are misrepresentative. It remains to be seen just how effective these counterappeals are.

What also remains to be seen is how effective arguments from just-war theory might be in presenting ethical or philosophic reasons to counter their opponents' arguments. So both on the factual and nonfactual levels, these theorists need not just argue defensively. Indeed, in theory, their counterattack might lead them to argue that their position is stronger now than in the past. We shall see whether this is so.

CHAPTER TWO

Modern Weaponry

What Is a Weapon?

Weapons can be talked about in narrow or broad terms. In the narrowest sense we can speak of something as a weapon only if it has the power to disable to destroy. In that sense, examples of weapons are bullets, explosive charges, poison gas, swords, sticks, and stones. In that same sense, a gun is not a weapon since it merely delivers the weapon to the target. Nor is a tracked vehicle a weapon, because it merely transports the gun, which in turn delivers the bullet (or shell) to the target. Nor finally is a gunsight a weapon, because it merely helps the gunner aim the gun.

This narrowest sense of "weapon" is not very useful for the purposes of this study because, for one thing, it is not in accord with the rather loose definition of "weapon" given in dictionaries. For example, *Webster's Ninth New Collegiate Dictionary* (1986) calls a weapon "an instrument of offense or defensive combat: something to fight with." For another, its very narrowness makes it more difficult to fully appreciate many of the recent changes on the battlefield. These changes range far beyond the disabling and destructive power of the war instruments that have been put into the hands of warriors by modern technology (Burke 1988, 50–60). Thus, to help gain some appreciation both of these changes and the profound effect they likely will bring to the battlefield of the future, the concept of weapon will be used here in a broad, perhaps even overly broad, sense.

In this study, weapons will be talked of primarily in terms of their functions. Swords, bullets, and explosives will thus count as weapons because their function or purpose is to disable or destroy. But by the broader characterization of what a weapon is, cannons and tanks will also count as weapons because they have a reaching function. To be sure, cannons possess this function more in the sense of delivering shells to the target, while tanks possess it more in the sense of transporting the cannon. Still, both instruments enable those who fight wars to reach out to the enemy forces in order to harm them. As weapons whose main function is to reach the enemy, such instruments as guns, cannon, mortar, rockets, bows, and sling shots all fall into the subcategory of delivery weapons, whereas such instruments as airplanes, trucks, tanks, naval vessels all fall into the subcategory of transport weapons.

Stretching the concept of weapons to include reach will not disturb most thinkers on the subject. But they might bridle some at hearing those instruments spoken of as weapons whose main function is to locate the enemy. Examples of locating instruments are gunsights, range finders, radar, sonar, thermal-imaging and light-enhancing devices, and binoculars. Locating instruments tell those using them that enemy forces are present (target acquisition), which ones are present (target discrimination), and where exactly they are located (target location). However, in part because these instruments are often even more remotely connected to bullets and bombs than are tanks and trucks, it is tempting not to think of them as weapons at all.

In the end, whether locating devices are counted as weapons or not is a terminological matter. They could be thought of as supportive instruments to the true weapons of war rather than weapons as such. But I will treat them as weapons in part because it is more convenient to do so, and in part because these instruments, more often than not, are tied too intimately to other kinds of weapons to deserve being singled out for separate treatment. In this sense, the gunsight seems too closely associated with the gun not to count as a weapon. So does the radar installation used to guide the surface-to-air missiles (SAMs). Homing devices on cruise missiles seem to be even more closely associated with that weapon's other functions to permit any separate treatment.

Another possibility is to think of locating devices as parts of total weapon systems, where such systems are thought of as combinations of weapons and other war instruments rather than as weapons. Although I find this terminology more acceptable as compared to not thinking of these instruments as weapons at all, I will stay with the somewhat expanded sense of the concept of weapon. A weapon, then, is any instrument whose function is to disable, reach, or locate the enemy (Fotion and Elfstrom 1986, 161–67). In contrast, a weapon system is any instrument that combines two or more of these kinds of instruments, possibly along with instruments (for example, radios) that have other valuable but nonweapon functions in war.

Having classified weapons in terms of their disabling, reaching, and locating functions, I need to point out that weapons do not always fall into just one category. Used in a karate chop, the human hand is a disabling weapon; used as a grenade holder, it is a reaching weapon. Similarly, the rifle is a reaching weapon primarily, but it is a disabling weapon when it is used to strike the enemy in hand-to-hand combat. In this same vein, an infantry-fighting vehicle can take guns and troops to battle or it can be used to run over and literally smash the enemy.

Nor should it be understood that this classification helps much in sorting some of the other important equipment found in and around the battlefield. Computers are good examples here, as are various communications systems. Are computers locating devices? Along with radar, they can be used that way, but they might also be used as aids in navigation and in that sense be thought of as aids to transportation and delivery weapons. Using computers as aids to disabling weapons seems more remote, but even here they could be (and are) used to program one rather than another type of explosion. And what about communications systems? A satellite communications link can be used to help in locating enemy forces, or at least inform others that they have been located. But it can also be used to guide various reaching forces toward their targets. The so-called command, control, communications, and intelligence forces (C^3I) of any military organization are not easy to classify.

One other problem in devising a useful classification system for weapons needs to be at least mentioned. Is the armor on a tank or a ship a weapon? What about the helmet worn by the soldier? Also what about electronic countermeasures used to confuse enemy missiles, airplanes, and other weapon systems? In other words, are those instruments employed in war for the purpose of protecting people and equipment spoken of properly as weapons? This is not an easy question to answer. Mainly for the sake of convenience, I will treat such defensive equipment as a fourth kind of weapon. However, nothing much in the discussion that follows rides on this rather arbitrary decision. The points I will make about defensive equipment would have the same force even if such equipment were classed as something other than weaponry.

Progress with Locating-type Weapons

It seems almost trite to say there has been spectacular progress in
weapons development during the last few decades and only somewhat
less trite to add that this progress cuts across all three forms of weaponry. Even so, because there is a general lack of appreciation for the
ways that weapons have improved recently, it makes sense to take a
closer look at some of these improvements. It also makes sense because
proponents of the big argument claim that these improvements will
make wars far more hellish than in the past. Our closer look will help in
assessing this claim.

Speaking in the most general terms and leaving the details for later,
I suggest that progress in the three kinds of weapons can be characterized as follows. In terms of locating weapons, progress has made it
possible to neutralize the four dimensions of distance, weather, time,
and inaccuracy. *Neutralizing* can most easily be explained by discussing
the dimension of distance first. When warships depended on eyesight
to spot enemy ships, location could be achieved at best only as far as
the horizon. When airplanes are used as scouts, location can be extended to hundreds of miles. With a spy satellite, enemy ships can, in
theory at least, be located no matter where they are. Thus, insofar as
spy satellites are not restricted in locating enemy forces by distance,
that dimension can be spoken of as having been neutralized. Whether
near or far, the enemy forces can be found.

In this same vein, modern locating weapons also neutralize weather.
So-called all-weather radar can spot the enemy in good and foul
weather, in or out of clouds and fog. Neutralizing time is a bit more
difficult to understand because it can be done two ways. Time can be
neutralized on a 24-hour basis. Thermal-imaging devices can locate
enemy patrols moving around in the dark. The imaging devices help to
locate them as they move closer to friendly lines. But time can also be
neutralized in a way that combines the functions of location with
communications. In the past, the enemy might have been located only
by means of photography, a technology that creates a gap of hours
before the film can be flown back to a base and developed. By then, of
course, the target might have moved or have been altered in some way.
So time is still a factor when this technology is used, even though it
represents an improvement over other cruder technologies. But time is
truly neutralized when location is presented on a real-time basis. When
a remotely piloted vehicle (RPV) equipped with a television camera
pictures enemy tanks in a certain faraway position, the enemy has been

located as being "there now." Time now has truly been neutralized in this locating and communicating sense.

Such real-time location, using television, laser beams, radar, and other devices, has also helped neutralize inaccuracy in hitting targets. As will be made clear shortly, there is more to overcoming inaccuracy than locating targets. Still, if targets cannot be located precisely, the chances of hitting them diminish greatly.

The claim that these four dimensions have been neutralized should not be misunderstood. What it amounts to is that, given modern locating (and communicating) technologies, neutralization *can* be achieved. This is not to say that it is easily achieved. The equipment required to do the job may not be available, if for no other reason than that it is very expensive. Or it may be available but not functioning properly. Another possibility is that the equipment is being misused by ill-trained or careless operators. Or, what is just as likely, the job is difficult because the enemy is employing countermeasures, such as defensive weaponry. The simple use of camouflage can foil locating procedures, either by making targets completely invisible, forcing enemy forces to use greater effort in locating targets, or misinforming them as to exactly where (or what) the targets are. On a more sophisticated level, radar jamming and stealth technologies built into aircraft can achieve the same results (Robinson 1987, 90–99).

Progress with Reaching-type Weapons

Moving to the reaching function of weaponry, again in the most general terms, improvements can be talked about along three dimensions: speed, distance, and precision. Most dramatically, we can see these improvements at work with ballistic missiles. In terms of speed and distance, they can move through near space many times the speed of sound so that practically any target on earth can be hit within 30 minutes. With these weapons, distance has been neutralized, and speed practically so. As to accuracy, or speaking more precisely, the tendency not to be accurate, that too is being neutralized. Improvement in ballistic-missile technology, through the use of terminal guidance, is getting to the point where these weapons can hit very small targets (individual buildings) even when fired from distances hundreds or thousands of miles away. In the near future, we may be talking about person-to-person deliveries.

These impressive developments in missile technology should not turn us away from other developments in the military's reach capabilities. What is impressive is not any one technology but the development across a broad range of technologies, all of which together herald major changes in how future wars probably will be fought. The following is a sample list. Similar to long-range ballistic missiles are short-range missiles and rockets that allow artillery to hit targets far beyond what they could using conventional shells. Here, for example, is what the U.S. Army's *1988–89 Green Book* says about its and NATO's MLRS (multiple-launch rocket system):

> MLRS is a free-flight artillery rocket system that greatly improves the conventional, indirect-fire capacity of the field Army. MLRS consists of a 12-round launcher mounted on a highly mobile, tracked vehicle and is capable of firing rockets one at a time or in rapid ripples to ranges of more than 30 kilometers. MLRS employs the "shoot and scoot" principle to limit vulnerability to counterbattery fire. In addition to the M77 dual-purpose conventional submunitions, the system can deliver the West German-developed AT2 scatterable mine warhead and has the potential for delivering other warheads, including "smart" munitions. The MLRS rocket is 13 feet long and nine inches in diameter. (P. 399)

The *Green Book* adds that the United Kingdom, West Germany, France, and the United States together are developing a terminally guided warhead for the MLRS, presumably to give it still more accuracy. In addition, development work is being done on the TACM (tactical missile system) so that when the MLRS is modified, it will enable NATO forces to reach "enemy second echelon forces at ranges beyond that of current cannon and rockets" (U.S. Army 1988, 401). The TACM's range may be on the order of 100, rather than 30, kilometers (*Jane's Defence Weekly*, December 16, 1989, 1321).

Also somewhat similar to missiles, in having a long reach and great accuracy, are cruise missiles. These small, low-flying missiles make it possible to extend the reach of a military power from just beyond the capability of normal artillery to almost half way around the world. Jet aircraft have these same reach capabilities and also have the advantage of being more flexible as to how they are deployed. Unlike cruise and ballistic missiles, they can be recalled or assigned alternative targets if necessary.

Helicopters extend the reach of the military in other ways. Although they are not as swift as most fixed-wing combat planes, and are vulnerable in high-technology war environments, they can not only attack with their own weapons but can also quickly land large numbers of military personnel and equipment behind enemy lines. These weapon systems, used in conjunction with other aircraft and missiles, truly can change how future wars will be fought. Their extensive use may make an anachronism of the notion of a relatively fixed battle line separating two opposing forces. Instead of looking in one direction for the enemy, soldiers will be looking for trouble all around them, even when they are one hundred or two hundred miles from what is supposed to be the front line (front edge of the battle area, or FEBA).

This tendency to be involved in fighting, even if one is supposedly not where the action is, has increased because of other developments in military technology. In World War I, armies moved into battle on foot, after being taken near the battle area by train. Even in World War II, armies fought and moved into battle on foot, although the development of the tank made it possible for a relatively small number of soldiers to get to the battle line without doing so on foot. But since World War II, armies have become thoroughly mechanized. This does not mean that much fighting will not be done on foot. Perhaps most of it still will be. But much of it will be done by whole units of soldiers who have been moved quickly up to and through FEBA by a variety of vehicles. This high mobility will add to the tendency for armies to face one another in any and all directions. In form, some land battles will resemble sea battles.

To appreciate better what improvements military technology has effected in reach, more needs to be said about accuracy. As has been noted already, overcoming inaccuracy is also a feature of weapons designed for locating the enemy. These weapons tell us with far greater precision just where and what the nature of the enemy is. In contrast, whether they are of the transportation or delivery variety, weapons concerned with reach can overcome imprecision by being able to maneuver into position after they have been given information about location. It does no good, even if radar tracks the enemy ships, if airplanes or missiles cannot maneuver into position to intercept an enemy. Such guidance requires a variety of technologies working together, not the least of which includes the use of computers to help assimilate incoming information and then to translate this information into directions for guiding missiles, airplanes, and other weapons to the target.

If the focus shifts more to the delivery rather than the transportation of reaching weapons, another dimension enters the picture, one concerned with the sheer quantity of destruction, or firepower, that can be unleashed in the enemy's direction. The most obvious example here is in rifle development. In World War I, the bolt-action rifle was the weapon of choice. It enabled soldiers to fire their weapons perhaps five or six times each minute. World War II saw the introduction of the semiautomatic and then the fully automatic rifle. Soon after the war, rifle soldiers had in their hands a weapon that could fire a clip of fifteen to twenty bullets in less than three seconds (Dunnigan 1983, 333). Increased firepower has helped the artillery even more. Some rocket launchers used by the Soviet army can fire over 700 rockets in less than 30 seconds as an effective way of supplementing the greater accuracy inherent in more traditional cannon (Dunnigan 1983, 79–80).

Sivard (1987, 15) helps give a further sense of the destructive power of modern weaponry: "The Browning machine gun which could fire 250 rounds per minute can now be replaced by a Minigun which fires 6,000 rounds per minute. The artillery shell which had a destructive area of 2,000 square meters gives way to a multiple launcher rocket system which can destroy an area of 500,000 square meters."

Progress with Disabling-type Weapons

All of us know that modern weapons have increased their disabling and destructive functions many times over in the last few decades. It is difficult not to focus attention on nuclear weapons, for we have been told that the nuclear weapons of the World War II era, which could individually do damage equivalent to what could be done by 350 B-29 bombers dropping conventional bombs, are mere toys by today's standards (Sivard 1987, 16–17). Modern nuclear warheads are quite commonly five, ten, twenty, and even more than one hundred times more powerful. Whereas a World War II nuclear warhead might have had the power equivalent to twenty thousand tons of TNT, some of the largest modern warheads have the power of eighteen million tons (eighteen megatons). And it is not just a question of the power of each weapon. We have been told also that the number of existing warheads means that a modern war fought with nuclear weapons cannot help but be radically different from past wars. One modern American Trident submarine can carry 24 ballistic missiles, each with eight warheads, and each warhead can carry a nuclear weapon having the equivalent power of one hundred thousand tons of TNT. This means that the explosive power built into one Trident submarine is almost one thousand times more than that of a single nuclear explosion of World War II. Now that the Trident is receiving the new, more powerful, and more accurate D-5 missile, its disabling function will increase even more. But there are, of course, many missile-bearing submarines—to be sure most not so capable as the Trident—and even more missiles based on land or carried on aircraft. When all the warheads found on these and other weapon systems (for example, bombs carried by tactical aircraft, artillery, mines, and so on) are counted, they add up to more than 50,000 (*Defense Monitor* 1988a, 5; 1988b, 2).

As impressive as statistics like these are, it would be quite misleading to focus on the revolution in nuclear weaponry alone in appreciating how military technology has made modern weapons more disabling and destructive. Conventional weaponry has witnessed its own revolution. Perhaps the most significant is in the area of submunitions. Submunitions are disabling weapons dispensed from a "mother" weapon. Cluster bombs represent one version of these weapons. With these bombs, a "mother" cannister can carry several hundred smaller bomblets (*Jane's Weapon Systems* 1988, 827–28). Because these bombs can be programmed to explode differentially when they hit "soft" or "hard" targets, one airplane making a single pass over a large target can do the damage it would have taken scores of airplanes to do in the past. Timing devices can also be put on these bombs so that, for example, if they land on an airfield, some will explode immediately while others will explode at different times. Some of these bombs are designed to penetrate concrete before exploding. Small, cheap, but very destructive plastic mines represent a related submunitions technology. They can be distributed by the hundreds of thousands and can be programmed in a variety of ways (for example, to explode after several or certain kinds of vehicles have passed over them). With submunitions it is not a matter of obtaining a bigger bang at one point, but doing far greater damage by multiplying the points where a bang occurs.

Fuel-air bombs can also be thought of as submunitions because they create an almost infinite number of points of explosion when they are detonated. When such bombs are dropped from an aircraft, they release a volatile mist, which is ignited at the right moment. The explosion has been compared to that of a small atomic bomb and is said to be three to five times more destructive than more conventional high explosives (Dunnigan 1983, 120).

Conventional bombs have also been improvements over the years. These improvements have not necessarily been dramatic, but they have led to bigger explosions relative to the weight of the weapon carried by an airplane. These improvements, in turn, have meant that aircraft can do more damage because they can carry a larger number of weapons.

One could go on listing how weapons have been improved in their ability to disable and destroy. Some that have not been mentioned thus far are intended to destroy tanks—as are depleted uranium shells, for example. These shells do their damage by burning through the tank's heavy armor rather than pushing or blasting their way through. Others have special antipersonnel characteristics, as do small shells that spread fléchettes (or darts) in all directions. Then there have been "improvements" in chemical and biological weapons. More on these later. But, by now, enough has been said to make it clear that disabling weaponry has indeed not lagged behind the other two basic kinds of weapons. Some of the improvements, as with the introduction of larger caliber weapons in artillery and tank guns, have followed the principle that bigger is better. As we have seen already, however, the principle often being followed is that more is better. This is the principle that animates the use of cluster bombs where hundreds of small disabling points are created instead of one big one. The disabling effect of one big explosion tends to fall off significantly the greater the distance is from the point of explosion (the disabling point). Cluster bombs tend to lessen this falloff significantly.

Where to Go from Here

This overview of modern weapons development has been primarily descriptive. Its intent has been to give the reader a sense of how a modern war would be fought using these weapons. In the next chapter, the focus shifts to ethics once more. With a better sense of what these weapons can do, and how they vary from one another, we are in a better position to look at the pacifists' big argument and at the realists' claim that ethics cannot be promulgated in modern wars. The next chapter, then, focuses on how the actual fighting of a modern war might be affected by these new weapons, for better or for worse. In the following chapters we will look at both pacifist and realist claims concerned not with the war itself but with the tendency modern weaponry has to trigger a war.

CHAPTER THREE

Jus in Bello and Modern Weaponry

Ethical Standards

"Weapons don't kill people, people kill people." We have all heard someone say something like this, sometime, somewhere. The point is that responsibility does not attach to objects but to people. Perhaps so. But it still makes sense to assess weapons in terms of whether they make the task of fighting an ethical war more or less difficult. Poison gas makes matters more difficult because it spreads its destructive effect over a wide area, in an almost random manner. That makes it difficult for those who use this weapon to disable the enemy without at the same time disabling many civilians as well. It may be that poison gas is also unethical for other reasons. The horrible way it kills people may be enough to condemn it as a weapon of war, especially since there are so many other effective ways to kill. Still, because poison gas is such a very crude area weapon, its use (forgetting for the moment that it is illegal) makes the task of commanders intent upon fighting ethical wars significantly more difficult.

In this regard, poison gas is not unique. The military arsenal contains a variety of area weapons, some more crude than others. But before examining whether some of these weapons make the military's job of pursuing a just-war policy prohibitively difficult, I will first discuss the ethical standards I will be appealing to in assessing the morality or immorality of certain weapons.

The big argument, it has been argued, is largely consequentialist in nature. According to the argument, modern wars have far more bad consequences than good ones. The costs in loss of life, suffering, loss of property, economic debt incurred in fighting a war, etc., are out of proportion to the benefits. In its extreme form, the big argument would be used by some unqualified pacifists to argue that no matter how worthy the goal might be, whether it is to punish an aggressor, make people free, or even restore peace, using war as a means to these goals can never be justified.

Although it is applied by pacifists to condemn all modern wars, this kind of argument is familiar to many just-war theorists because it appeals to the so-called proportionality principle. In its crudest form, this principle states that the actions chosen should seek a balance of benefits over harms, all things considered. Just-war theorists use the proportionality principle to decide which wars give benefits of a certain sort, and therefore are just; and which do not, and therefore are not. In contrast, at least some pacifists also use the proportionality principle, shaped now as the big argument, to argue that all modern wars are unjust. The difference between the just-war theorists and pacifists at this point is therefore not a matter of principle but of calculation. This is what I meant in chapter 1 when I said that the big argument is based on empirical considerations—on our experiences with war and modern military organizations—rather than simply on abstract principles of right and wrong.

Of course, it could be argued that the calculations that would help decide which side is closer to the mark cannot be made, and that to make out their case both sides would be better off appealing solely to abstract religious, philosophic, and ethical principles. As stated in chapter 1, these kinds of appeals are being ignored in this study. Aside from the fact that they have their own problems, it is significant that the temptation to look toward consequences is almost irresistible. Even after we have been told the overall difficulties inherent in assessing consequences because of the specific difficulties of making interpersonal comparisons and of comparing various kinds of goods, we still find ourselves making consequentialist calculations. We read, for instance, that Emperor Wu, an ancient Chinese emperor in the Han dynasty, fought a war that cost thousands of lives, for the purpose of adding some rare horses to his stable (Creel 1953, 167–68). With the information given us and with the proportionality principle, we can easily calculate that he must have initiated an unjust war. It has been argued that Alexander the Great's wars are similarly unjust insofar as they left a "trail of rapine, slaughter, and subjugation" for what seems to us today little else than a desire to satisfy a gigantic ego (Green 1970, 260). In the same vein, we can easily calculate that launching a major war to punish those responsible for occasional sniper fire across the border is a disproportionate response. So there is little question that consequences can be and are assessed in accordance with something like the proportionality principle. To be sure, it will quickly become obvious that assessing wars fought for horses or to stop sniper fire is a lot easier than assessing the morality of many modern wars. Still, people make such assessments, and the task of this work is to see, finally, whether these assessments make sense; and, if they do, which ones make the most sense.

The proportionality principle is not the only one that the proponents and opponents of the big argument appeal to in defending their position. The discrimination principle is also at work here. We have already come across this principle in the pacifist complaint that modern wars will kill too many innocent lives (chapter 1). Indirectly, an appeal to this principle was also made insofar as area weapons were mentioned in this and the previous chapter. Simply put, the discrimination principle assesses the morality of a war, or actions in a war, in terms of how well the harm done by war separates participants from nonparticipants. If a bombing raid in the middle of a war kills nothing but soldiers and destroys nothing but military equipment, it would be just—other things being equal. Instead, if it kills nothing but people who have nothing to do with the war, it would be unjust—other things being equal.

Several comments about this principle are in order. First, the discrimination principle can be derived from the proportionality principle, but it need not be. Consequentialist thinkers probably feel more favorably inclined toward such a derivation because they can argue that participants in war have different preferences than do nonparticipants. Although members of neither group want to become casualties in war, the former group's preferences include a willingness to fight, whereas the latter group's preferences do not. For consequentialists, then, killing and maiming a war's participants, as opposed to its nonparticipants, is a lesser evil.

Nonconsequentialists tend not to fancy this argument. If anything, they would place the discrimination principle over the proportionality principle. They might do this for a variety of reasons, among them being that the rights of nonparticipants or the duties we have toward them take precedence over the calculations of good and bad consequences. For the purposes of this study, there is no need to take sides on this issue. Whatever the ultimate status of these principles, they can both be treated as important by all sides because disagreements in theory about these matters do not necessarily (and in fact often do not) yield disagreements about the validity of the big argument.

Second, the discrimination like the proportionality principle is a just-war principle primarily because it can be used to help tell us on which side of the just/unjust line we wish to place a bombing raid, an attack, or a whole war. At best, pacifists will be comfortable appealing to this principle in their backup arguments, and at worst be uncomfortable with it. Absolute pacifists, especially, will have these reservations simply because they condemn all human killing so strongly. Having done so, they cannot easily muster up an even stronger vocabulary to condemn the killing of women and children. If it is already an absolute wrong to kill soldiers, is killing innocent women and children a double absolute wrong? What can such double-talk mean? Whatever it does, if pacifists are to make sense of the discrimination principle in their big argument, they must be able to say something like this. It may be possible for them to do this, but it is not easy.

Third, in discussing the principles of proportionality and discrimination, I am not necessarily prejudicing the presentation against the realists. It might seem otherwise because both these principles fall inside ethics, while realism falls outside. However, these principles are being discussed on a conditional basis. The argument says that if one of the opposing ethical positions is correct, it is these principles to which these two theories would most likely be appealing in attempting to assess the big argument. So the principles of proportionality and discrimination are being discussed by way of helping to explain the two ethical theories rather than as a way of pushing the realist arguments off the discussion table. The realist arguments will be dealt with in due time.

On the Negative Side

I have already argued that although people are ultimately responsible for the use of weapons, some weapons seem to be inherently more negative, or are more immoral than others. Because of its crudity as an area weapon, poison gas seems to fall into the immoral category. Indeed, because of modern war conditions, the use of poison gas is more likely to fall into the immoral category than it did in World War I. The static nature of that war and the limited reach of the contesting forces meant that the poison gas affected military personnel almost exclusively. The battle area was so worked over that civilians had long since left the scene. In that war, gas, as an uncontrollable area weapon, was more likely to reach back to affect its users than affect civilians. That scenario is not likely to hold in a major war of the future. Because opposing forces may use missiles and airplanes to reach deep behind

FEBA, winds will likely carry the deadly gas into farms, villages, towns, and cities still occupied by many civilians. Unlike World War I, it will be more difficult in a major future war for commanders to avoid significant violations of the discrimination principle if they use poison gas. Not only are they more likely to violate this principle because of how things will be in the next war, but they will also have the opportunity to violate it intentionally. With modern delivery systems, poison gas could more readily be used directly against civilian populations than it was in World War I. In particular, it could be used against villages in remote areas where it is more difficult to prove to the outside world that such a weapon was actually used.

In their own way, if many of the newer submunitions were used extensively, they too would make the job of fighting an ethical war more difficult. Cluster bombs dispensed in a major war on a highway taking military personnel toward the battle and civilians from it will certainly also challenge the discrimination principle. So will the random use of plastic mines deep behind FEBA. If poison gas is to be condemned because of its crudity as an area weapon, it would seem that these other area weapons would also have to be condemned.

However, it is difficult to marshal enough arguments to draw this conclusion convincingly. Part of the reason for this is just that poison gas can be labeled immoral for more than its crudity as an area weapon. Because poison gas horrifies people more than other weapons, they are more willing to label it an immoral weapon. Yet it is not clear, for example, that death by poison gas is more painful than death by shrapnel. Both can bring on death instantaneously, or painfully by degrees. Is poison gas more horrifying because we can imagine death by this means more dramatically? Is it more horrifying because we envision it as a destroyer of life without so much as scratching any real estate? Or because it is such an insidious, silent killer? Whatever the case, cluster bombs and modern plastic mines look too much like weapons we are already familiar with for these weapons to have the same emotional impact on us. So it is easier to accept them than poison gas, even if they do as much or more area damage than poison gas does.

Another reason cluster bombs and modern plastic mines cannot be morally condemned carte blanche is that we can imagine many legitimate uses for them. Imagine the enemy forming with an overwhelming array of mechanized forces, including main battle tanks, armored personnel carriers, and artillery. To attack, these forces must move through a fairly narrow plain, and it seems obvious that they will do so quickly unless they are slowed in some way. Two ways to slow them are to throw thousands of plastic mines in their path before they move in and then drop cluster bombs on them as they move through. A variety of similar scenarios can be imagined, where it is clear that the submunitions revolution enables military forces to perform traditional tasks more quickly and effectively than they have been able to do in the past. The same can be said for fuel-air weapons. They can be used to slow the advance of the enemy's overwhelming mechanized forces, but also to destroy minefields and clear landing areas for helicopters.

Still, doubt remains. "Yes," pacifists (and others) will reply, "these are familiar weapons and, yes, they can be used in legitimate ways, but the temptation either to overuse or misuse them will be great. If major modern wars are going to be chaotic affairs, as almost everybody supposes they will be, having such weapons in hand cannot help but lead to all sorts of violations of the principle of discrimination and even possibly the principle of proportionality. It is all well and good to piously encourage military commanders and warriors to use these weapons with care. It is quite another thing to realistically expect them to do so. Besides, what can 'use these weapons with care' mean when civilians are mixed with military forces? In such settings either one uses these weapons or one does not. If one does, many civilians will die along with the soldiers; if one doesn't, then it is more likely that the enemy forces will break through our lines or escape. These are the weapons of the butcher, not the surgeon."

This pacifist argument is powerful. But it can be carried one step further and thereby made even more powerful. "Those in favor of retaining these weapons in military arsenals argue that it would be difficult to banish these weapons from the battlefield. Part of their argument is that, now that we have them, it would be difficult to monitor compliance if these weapons were to be banned or some limit put on their manufacture or deployment. But if we grant this to be so, and if we couple it with the conclusion of the previous paragraph that it would be extremely difficult to use these weapons morally, it follows that it would be extremely difficult to fight any major modern war morally. In short, given modern technology, we pacifists are right. Modern wars not only are, but cannot help but be, immoral."

I will leave this argument against the use of submunitions as it is for now. As I said, it is powerful and is, in fact, a detailed working out of a part of the big argument. I will attempt to give a final assessment of it when the likely roles of other weapons in future wars have been characterized. Indeed, I want to turn to some of these other weapons now, in particular to the use of high-mobility weapons such as helicopters, airplanes, mechanized army units, and the like.

It should be obvious that basically the same arguments pacifists use against weapons of the submunitions revolution apply here as well. These weapons too are nothing more than refined instruments with which we have all been familiar throughout the twentieth century. Helicopters are somewhat newer than most of these weapons, but even they have been around for about half of this century. So when generals tell us they cannot do without helicopters, fixed-wing aircraft, tanks, mechanized troop carriers, and mobile artillery units made up of both gun and rocket units, automatic rifles, and the like, pacifists can argue once again that modern war has become immoral through and through. That is, it is not as if all we need to do in order to make modern wars moral again is outlaw a few isolated, nasty weapons. Across the board, their argument is, weapons have just become too powerful to be used in any morally acceptable way in war.

If more support for their general position is needed, pacifists need only point to those weapons standing in the wings ready to go on war's center stage should nations lose all their sense of sanity. Should one side in a war become desperate, nuclear weapons, poison gas, and biological weapons could all be used. And the effect would predictably be to make wars that are already immoral (from the pacifist point of view) more thoroughly so.

Pacifists have still another argument to clinch their case. Most generally, this argument appeals to the proportionality principle more than to the discrimination principle, but it specifically appeals to economic considerations. The negative disproportionate consequences of a war, the pacifists tell us, should not be identified simply as those concerned with the fighting itself. Lives lost and maimed are part of the calculation, but so are the economic costs of war. And, the pacifists remind us, modern high-technology wars are so costly that even victorious nations, no matter how rich they are, court economic disaster if they become involved in such wars. We will look at this argument, concerned as it is with deterring wars, in greater detail in later chapters. For now, it is enough to note that aside from deterrence, both the short- and long-run economic costs of war need to be figured into the calculations concerned with whether the war is being fought in a proportionate manner or not. About that, the pacifists are right. Whether they are right that these costs are inevitably backbreaking economically remains to be seen.

On the Neutral Side

The destructive power of a weapon should not be automatically equated negatively with morality. The fact that a modern tank can destroy another tank efficiently because, among other reasons, it can shoot effectively on the run (as it could not in World War II), does not mean that it is a more immoral weapon. The variation of the big argument presented in the previous section does not, as such, focus on the greater killing power of these weapons when it concludes that they make modern wars immoral. Rather, the main focus is on lack of discrimination. But insofar as the big argument has this focus, it becomes possible for killing power to be thought of as neutral morally if it discriminates between those who should and should not be shot at. That is, if army A thoroughly destroys army B in part because it has superior equipment, it is neither more nor less immoral than B. To be sure, the principle of proportionality could come into play in such a situation. If A not only soundly defeats B but lays casualties on its enemy by using its superior technology far beyond the point of defeating B, then A is acting immorally. It is no longer battling but, instead, slaughtering B. But insofar as army A uses laser-guided weapons, remotely piloted vehicles (RPVs), advanced attack helicopters, and other high-technology weapons not available to B to bring about the defeat, morality is not being abused. As it might be put, ethics is silent here.

This point needs to be clarified. Imagine the commander of army A reviewing in his own mind the results of the battle. No doubt he feels good that his side won, yet feels bad that his side suffered numerous casualties. If he is a sensitive soul, he will also be upset that army B's casualties were horrendous. Overall, he might be depressed to the point of asking himself whether he did anything wrong morally. The answer he himself (and others) most likely would give is "No, I (you) did nothing wrong—even though people died, and even though I (you) had much to do with bringing about these deaths."

But is doing nothing wrong in this and similar settings still a matter of acting within a moral framework? And if it is, how can ethics be silent in this situation?

A distinction needs to be made at this point. Ethics is not silent when the battle is described in any number of ways. For the commander (and all those under him), there are decisions to be made that can result in moral condemnation and praise. In this sense, acting in war is no different from acting on a daily basis during peacetime. The main difference is that some of the major ethical rules have been "relaxed" severely during wartime. Even so, from the just-war tradition, there are rules, principles, etc., that can be violated during war. Insofar as there is ethics, it can speak about actions as wrong, not wrong, and even as right. Concerning the latter, for example, the commander can be said to have rightly done his duty in conscientiously working to bring about the victory for army A.

In this connection, he also has done his military and moral duties in effectively deploying and using the weapons his nation has given him and his troops. In contrast, he would have been derelict both militarily and morally if he had not used these weapons and thereby suffered a defeat. So if we view the battle as a whole and also view it from the commander's responsibilities to his troops (and the causes for which he fights), ethics can speak loudly. But if we view high-technology weapons simply as more effective instruments of destruction, the commander's use of them is neither moral nor immoral. Other things being equal, it makes no difference morally if he destroys the enemy with one shot or one hundred.

It is important to understand this point because loose talk about the greater destructive power of modern weapons might lead one to condemn modern weaponry carte blanche. Modern antitank weapons undoubtedly are better killers than their World War II predecessors. But such weapons need to be sharply distinguished from such morally suspect weapons as cluster bombs. Although these weapons are also better killers than their World War II counterparts, their problem, as we have seen, is that they are poor discriminators of those who are and those who are not participants in war.

The point about the relatively neutral moral status of certain weapons is also important because antitank weapons are not the only "neutral" weapons found on the battlefield. The weapons that tend to be neutral are those specialized in hitting and defending strictly military targets. In fact, there are plenty of those around. In addition to antitank weapons, there are antiship, antiaircraft, and antimissile weapons. Then there is a wide range of weaponry to defend against such attacks. Indeed, much weaponry is designed and is employed almost exclusively to deal with strictly military targets. Indirectly, these weapons might still be said to be immoral because they drain resources that might better be spent in other ways. But directly, their employment is neither here nor there morally.

A disclaimer is in order here. Even morally neutral weapons can be used immorally. Antitank weapons can be aimed at civilian buildings just as air-to-air missiles can be aimed at civilian airliners. That is obvious. The point in calling these weapons morally neutral is not that they cannot be used immorally. Rather, it is that these weapons are usually used on strictly military targets if for no other reason than many of them are too expensive to be deployed against everyday civilian targets.

On the Positive Side

Just as some weapons tend to be morally suspect and others tend to be neutral, still other weapons tend to make modern wars more acceptable. That is, their employment makes it possible for military forces to fight wars that are more moral than those fought in the past. A laser-guided bomb dropped on a bridge that happens to be in the middle of a village full of civilians is a big improvement over a free-falling iron bomb that, more than likely, would hit the village rather than the bridge when released from a World War II aircraft, let alone a fast-flying jet. The military's ability to neutralize imprecision both with respect to location and reach (and with respect to transportation and delivery) allows for significant discrimination between those that should and those that should not be targeted.

These forms of accuracy are potentially helpful morally for a wide variety of targets. Finding, locating precisely, identifying, and reaching out with precision are helpful skills in destroying clusters of small and large military forces and facilities, munitions, and other military-related factories, railroad yards, communications facilities, and other such targets, all while putting those who should not be involved in war at minimal risk. This does not mean that these skills will actually be employed properly. The skills to hit and only hit a military airport are after all the same as those needed to hit and only hit a hospital. It also does not mean that those who possess these weapons will know how to use them properly. Least of all does it mean that, in the chaos of battle, the accuracy inherent in modern weapons would enable wars to be fought "surgically." What it means is that these weapons make at least a somewhat morally cleaner war possible. The cleanliness here is not just with respect to those people who are not supposed to be involved in the war, but also with respect to the environment. To get a certain job done, the military need not destroy both the enemy and his surroundings; it is now possible for it to take out only the enemy.

So far, greater accuracy with respect to location and reach has been seen to be a step in the right direction morally in connection with the discrimination principle. But accuracy speaks positively to the proportionality principle as well. Proportionality, it will be recalled, is mainly a quantitative principle. It is often applied in just-war theory in dealing with *jus ad bellum* problems. Thus, a costly war to avenge a small harm is said to be unjust by this principle. In the same vein, during war it would be disproportionate to destroy a purely military target by expending much life and material when the job could be done with one or two small "smart" weapons. Of course, "smart" weapons may in some cases be more expensive overall because of the high costs of the electronics necessary to make them so intelligent. But in many other cases, the opposite is the case. In World War II scores of shells had to be fired in the process of destroying one tank. Now the job can often be done by firing one or two missiles at most. Thus, the above-mentioned process of destroying the bridge through the use of laser beams not only saves civilian lives but also the lives and resources of the attacking nation.

In a way, this is a strange argument because it suggests that the more efficient the military on side A becomes in destroying the military on side B, the more moral it is. It just seems counterintuitive to say anything like this. But if we assume that the war side A is fighting is moral that therefore it is fitting and proper for it to do what it can to destroy the military forces of B, it is also fitting and proper for A to do its job without squandering the people and resources on its side. Some of the battles of World War I were condemned just because of the great waste of men and material. Thousands of lives were lost in attempts, usually futile, to take a line or two of trenches. It was not the taking of the trenches in itself that was immoral. Rather, it was the cost in lives and material. If new weapons help us avoid these costs, then having and using them have to represent steps in the right direction.

This conclusion could be countered by reminding us that side B can also use these same smart weapons. If it is proper for A to use them for the reason given, then B has every right to use them as well. Admittedly this is right. But then, one might wonder, where has the alleged moral progress inherent in using modern weapons gone? What gain has been registered morally when both sides get technologically efficient at killing one another?

Perhaps none. It may be that technology acts in some situations simply to neutralize things morally. Still, even if both sides possess smart weapons, certain uses of these weapons where one side has an advantage will save lives; and insofar as it does, some gain will be registered. The gain, of course, will be elusive. Technological fixes can slip out of a country's grasp quickly. It nonetheless seems correct to say that those commanders who do what they can to provide their forces with technologically superior weapons are doing their duty, while those who do not, are not.

All this may be controversial. It may be that I am just wrong in supposing that technology can be seen as improving the moral setting of war by helping military people kill and maim others more efficiently, and in the process protecting themselves from assault. Much less controversial is the moral gain of what can be called a military's reach-back capability. Enough has already been said about the greater reach modern weapons have over those of even three or four decades ago. But some reaching weapons can work in both directions. Helicopters, especially, can both reach out and reach back quickly (Keegan and Holmes 1986, 153). In reaching back, they can perform a great humanitarian service of saving the lives of those who have been wounded in battle. Statistics show that in Vietnam, facilities among wounded soldiers were cut down significantly because helicopters, as well as other modes of rapid transportation, got those wounded back to where they could receive medical attention, often in a matter of minutes. Lives were saved as well because medical technology has advanced far in the past few decades. Together, reach back and better quality medicine meant that for U.S. soldiers "a wounded man's chances were better than ever before: only 1% of wounded reaching a medical facility died, a figure which compares favourably with the 2.2% in Korea and 4.5% in the Second World War" (Keegan and Holmes 1986, 154). There is no doubt that the low death rate figures for Vietnam would have been higher if the Vietcong could have challenged the Americans in the sky. A war fought between the United States and the Soviet Union would undoubtedly raise the death figures among the wounded. Nonetheless, basically the same technology that can be used to raise havoc behind enemy lines and create moral problems (discussed earlier in this chapter) can also help improve the moral setting of war.

If anything, this technology will likely be extended. Like helicopters, vertical takeoff planes, such as the United States' V22, or so-called Osprey, can perform similar reach-out and reach-back tasks but can perform them with greater speed and range (Famiglietti and Beaver 1988, 1095). Larger, more conventional planes (for example, America's C-17), with landing and takeoff capabilities from less-than-ideal airstrips, can also be used to bring wounded back quickly from the battlefield (Wrixon 1986, 965–69). Also, ground-based mechanized forces, the same ones that attack enemy forces deep behind FEBA, can be used to reach back and bring casualties to medical centers faster than before.

Countermeasures, Counter-Countermeasures, et Cetera

It is not completely clear how all these negatives, neutrals, and positives would balance out were a high-technological, nonnuclear war to get under way near the end of this century and the beginning of the next. All things considered, would things be morally worse than in a war that might have taken place in 1960? Or worse than World War II? Some would argue that it would be, and they would do so simply by focusing on the awesome nature of fuel-air bombs, various kinds of submunitions, and the increased firepower in the hands of infantry, artillery, and airborne forces. Others would argue just the opposite. They would do so by focusing not only on such positive factors as those noted above but also on the weapons of modern war that have received only cursory attention in this study up to now: countermeasure or defensive weapons.

Countermeasures can take many forms. Against helicopters and other low-flying, fixed-wing aircraft, they can be in the form of hand-held missiles (like the United States' Stinger and Great Britain's Blowpipe) or more powerful SAMs (surface-to-air missiles). Just putting these kinds of weapons in the hands of the Afghanistan rebels forced Soviet helicopters and aircraft to fly at higher altitudes and thus become much less effective in destroying rebel forces, supplies, and villages. Against tanks, there are powerful antitank weapons; and then against these weapons are new forms of armor (more on these later) to protect the tank. Also against locating weapons such as radar, there are antiradiation weapons. These weapons use the radar signals sent by an attacking aircraft to identify where the attacker is located. Antiradiation weapons can also be used to attack SAMs that use radar to identify the location of attacking aircraft. So we have here measures taken to attack an enemy, countermeasures against such an attack, countermeasures against the countermeasures, and so on.

It is in large part the net effect of these measures and countermeasures that makes it difficult to know what will happen once a major high-technology war begins in the near future (Burke 1988, 51–52). Those who argue that the net effect would not be so devastating do so because they figure that these measures and countermeasures might just cancel each other out, which is a real possibility. Another possibility is that even if one side does not have an overwhelming advantage in quantity or quality of equipment (and the personnel to use it effectively), a canceling would not take place. The argument here seems to be that small advantages in electronic warfare can have a magnifying effect on the battlefield. The most recent war between the Israelis and the Syrians over the issue of Lebanon serves as an example. The Israeli electronic advantage was such that they won an overwhelming victory in the air. Yet before the war started, it was not a foregone conclusion that the Israelis would win such a victory, because the Syrians were not lacking in their own sophisticated equipment.

In fact, theories abound when it comes to predicting what would happen if two highly technological forces met head-on in a conventional war. As noted earlier, decades have passed since superpowers have met in an all-out war. It is therefore impossible to know who is right here. About the only thing one can be sure of is that this war, whether totally devastating or not, would be terribly expensive. Committing weapons of thrust and counterthrust to battle would be a way of throwing away national treasures at a rate unheard of in any previous war.

CHAPTER FOUR

Deterrence

Looking back at the Big Argument

One aspect of the big argument is that modern weapons do not deter war. Just the opposite, they cause war. A second aspect of this argument is that because of the power and quick-strike potential of modern weaponry, nations have been forced to maintain large standing military forces, which, in turn, also do not act as deterrents. Instead, they too cause wars. In the past, so the argument goes, the state raised armies and navies to achieve some offensive or defensive goal. Once they were raised, there was always the temptation to say, "Let us find some use for these forces." But modern military forces do not have to be raised. By and large, they are always in place, so the temptation to use them is always present.

It is difficult to know how to assess this latter aspect of the big argument. It certainly sounds plausible, and one can cite historical examples where armies and navies were used in part because they existed. Late in the sixteenth century, Japan found uses for its military professionals in Korea (Han 1970, 268–70). Toyotomi Kideyoshi, the ruler of Japan at that time, apparently needed to find work overseas for the samurai once the civil wars in his country had subsided. It would not do to have them roaming the Japanese countryside causing trouble. Better that they be roaming elsewhere. More than three centuries later, World War I was, according to some writers, partly caused by the armaments race and by military forces seemingly looking for work in neighboring lands (King 1972, xx–xxi; Taylor 1963, 12–13). Certainly, if these military forces were not in place, these wars would not have ensued. Still, in some cases, wars came about not because military forces were in place but because they were put there to make war. So although the mere presence of military forces might sometimes cause wars, it is not so clear how often this happens.

What further complicates the situation is that others have developed an argument directly opposed to the big argument. The argument is almost as old as civilization. Mo Tzu appealed to it and then acted in accordance with it about twenty-five hundred years ago. He deterred the King of Ch'u from invading Sung by placing his small but determined and well-organized band of followers in harm's way (Fung 1952, 81). Much more recently, and more famously, many have argued that World War II might not have taken place had the Western powers possessed military forces to deter Adolf Hitler. Thus, even if in-place military forces sometimes seem to cause war, at other times they seem to prevent it.

On the Negative Side

However, the task in this chapter is not to look at the causes of war and peace throughout history, although it might be illuminating to do that as well. Rather, it is to look at the possibilities of war and peace in the near future, possibilities that, because of modern technology, might pose opportunities and threats unique in history.

Most of the arguments on the negative, war-causing side appeared in chapter 1 in the process of introducing the big argument. But two points need more emphasis to show more clearly why deterrence is supposed to be such an inappropriate policy in these modern times.

First, deterrence policies themselves are said to be more dangerous today than in the past. Under the best of circumstances, carrying out such policies is like a balancing act featuring two ungainly performers who, if left alone with their own limitations, might pull off their act. But modern times, it is also said, do not represent the best of circumstances. Factors mentioned already all work in one direction to destabilize any attempts at deterrence. These include the influences of those who make up the world's military-industrial complexes, whose interests often conflict with those of national welfare. They also include the quick-strike potential and greater destructive capability of modern weaponry. Together, these factors make those attempting to achieve deterrence more trigger happy and therefore more likely to fail.

Second, deterrence policies unfortunately must rely upon constant technological fixes to maintain the desired balance. In the past, when the technology of war moved slowly, the fixes could be made leisurely. But in today's frenetic high-technology world, nations cannot afford to get too far behind in first one and then another area of military preparedness. What was a lead a year or so ago can, if a nation is not careful, represent a bad second-place position today. To be sure, the lead can change again in another year or so, but that shows how fleeting security is in modern times.

That technological leads can be so fleeting should not surprise. After all, modern technology is so difficult to hide that technological overlapping, brought about by hard work, reading the other side's public documents, spying, and other means, inevitably will be the norm. If two opposing nations are close technologically and are equal in economic power and in the size of their military establishment, it is easy to imagine how vast amounts of money could be spent by each side to stay even. If, as in the case of the conflict between the United States and the Soviet Union, economic and technological factors favor the former but size of the military establishment favors the latter, a balancing of quality against quantity will likely ensue. Even with a quantitative advantage in such things as military personnel, tanks, artillery, air-planes, and helicopters, the USSR cannot afford to get too far behind qualitatively. So whether or not the two sides are equal in high technology, an expensive race is inevitable. Also inevitable, because the race will be fought on such a broad front of technologies, will be the difficulty in assessing who is ahead and, more important, whether a balance has been achieved that will allow deterrence to work (Stubbing 1987, 65; *Soviet Military Power* 1988, 149).

On the Neutral and Positive Sides

Those who would argue against these pacifist arguments need not deny all of what the arguments say. They can grant that modern military technology is fast moving and that much of what is loosely called the arms race is a rat race. They need not even deny the dangers inherent in having military-industrial complexes around permanently. Nor need they deny that modern weapons have greater quick-strike potential and are more devastating than weapons created twenty and thirty years ago. All this can be granted. What they need not grant is that all modern technology works in the direction of making deterrence less viable. Indeed, some just-war theorists would oppose these pacifist arguments by insisting that any carte blanche condemnation of modern military technology is too simplistic. They would insist that a careful look at modern weapon types, either individually or by group, is necessary to determine how that technology affects both the fighting of the war itself and the tendency these weapons have to tempt nations to go to war. In fact, that is the approach being taken in this study.

Certainly, one technology these just-war theorists would point to is location. Both pacifists and nonpacifists alike have argued that wars have often been triggered by misinformation about the enemy's intentions and capabilities. Allegedly, nations have blundered into war because they overestimated the threats some nations posed or underestimated other nations' strengths. If this is so, modern locating devices such as surveillance satellites can mitigate the amount of misinformation (Tsipis 1987, 79–93). During war, these same satellites can be used to help missiles find their targets. And during peacetime, they can be used profitably to plan for a war of aggression. It is convenient to know where the enemy forces are located just before you make an effort to destroy them. So the suggestion here is not that these weapon systems serve only to maintain peace. Still, during peacetime and while in the hands of those trying to avoid war, these satellites can lessen the misinformation that can lead to war.

Some pacifists might reply that the contributions satellites make to peace are hardly very comforting. They will note that these satellites can be used to locate enemy forces in planning an offensive war and add that this use fits right into their claim that modern wars cannot help but be trigger-sensitive affairs. Modern surveillance satellites give aggressors just the instruments of war they need to enable them to use their quick-strike forces most effectively. It would be better, these pacifists might add, if these weapons simply did not exist.

Two brief comments are in order. First, this last sentiment is quixotic. The cliché usually cited to drive this point home is that "you can't put the genie back into the bottle." Indeed, you cannot, because the knowledge and skills associated with putting surveillance and other kinds of satellites in space are too public to be suppressed. Too many people in too many nations with too many different political and social outlooks have the know-how and resources to put satellites in space to put these technologies away.

The second comment is less obvious but equally true. When all is said and done, we probably do not want to put the genie away. The sentiment for putting it away gains most of its credibility when we think of military satellites or think of all the other military technologies. Those with this sentiment want to get rid of the nasty war technologies but keep the nice peaceful ones. But, to a large extent, this is a false dichotomy. Some war technologies are specialized. Making tanks, large guns, bombs, mines, and aircraft carriers requires specialized technologies not matched in civilian living. Many of these technologies probably never would have been developed had war not been a rather common human pastime. Still, many technologies of war have so much in common with those of peace that it is hard to imagine how the one could be suppressed without suppressing the other. The technologies of reach and location required to find an enemy aircraft carrier at sea from several hundred miles in space are not so different from those useful in locating natural resources in the ground or monitoring crop conditions on earth. Similarly, military airplanes, helicopters, trucks, radar, sonar, and engines of all kinds have their rough counterparts in the civilian area.

The defenders of the big argument would find none of this comforting. Admitting that the genie cannot be bottled does not make the situation less dangerous. In the hands of potential aggressors, they will say, these satell:tes will make it more likely that aggressive wars will be successful.

Very likely this would be right if the potential victim of aggression did not possess surveillance satellites of its own. What more could a potential aggressor want, besides a strong and swift-striking military force, than to know exactly where the enemy is located—without the victim's knowing where its forces are located? But to grant this much to pacifists unhappy with surveillance satellites is only to concede that any weapon of war could be used for some evil purpose. Deterrence theorists need not deny this point either. What they should be concerned with denying is that these satellites have no deterring effects when they are in the hands of nonaggressor nations. Deterrence theorists are saying that when nonaggressor nations have these locating technologies available to them, they can, at worst, take steps to blunt the aggressor's attack. Speaking more to the topic of this chapter, however, they can add that these satellites can actually help deter war. Indeed, it is difficult to see how the deterrent theorists could be wrong about this. Because the potential aggressor would know that its victim's satellites are in place, it could hardly expect its surprise attack to actually surprise anyone.

But beyond having a deterring effect on imminent war, these satellites permit nations to monitor each other over the long haul. They lessen the chances of potential aggressor nations gradually building up their military forces and then surprising other nations with overwhelming power and new technologies. Modern weapons, as we have seen, allow for surprise attacks because of their quick-strike potential. But modern weapons also require long gestation periods, thereby giving surveillance satellites ample opportunity to anticipate their birth.

Other satellites are less directly able to play deterrent roles, but even some of these can do so to some extent. By and large, however, they can best be spoken of as neutral with respect to deterrence and nondeterrence. On the one hand, these satellites help such weapons as submarine-launched ballistic missiles (SLBMs) achieve greater accuracy by helping submarines precisely determine their position. To that extent, satellites make it possible for submarines to be used in a war of aggression to destroy such things as the victim nation's communications, control, command, and intelligence (C^3I) functions. In the parlance of modern war, these satellites could help the aggressor nation decapitate its victim. On the other hand, navigation satellites also help make decapitating counterstrikes possible. Knowing that it can be hurt fatally, even after it has hurt a victim nation fatally, might just have a strong deterrent effect on an aggressor nation. We will examine this form of deterrence more when the discussion turns to nuclear weapons in the next chapter.

Communications satellites have a similar neutral role with respect to deterrence and nondeterrence. Like navigation satellites, communications satellites are important for both aggressors and victims. Excellent communications enable the aggressor to coordinate worldwide quick-strike attacks, but at the same time communications systems (if they survived the initial attack) aided by satellites could make a coordinated counterstrike possible. Again, knowing that victim nations can still maintain communications links with aircraft, submarines, surface ships, and distant military outposts after being devastated by a first-strike attack likely will have a sobering effect on any nation contemplating aggression.

Some Other Defensive Weapons

Two obvious, but nonetheless effective, counterarguments might be forthcoming from pacifist circles at this point. The first can be expressed as follows. "In the end, even if we grant that surveillance satellites serve an important deterrent function, and that a few other weapons are neutral with respect to that function, this is hardly going to change the thrust of our overall argument about the general nondeterrent nature of modern weaponry. As against this one (allegedly) deterrent weapons system, there are a host of systems starting with nuclear-armed intercontinental ballistic missiles (ICBMs) all the way down to a wide variety of automatic small arms that cannot help but be viewed as more nondeterring than deterring in nature. No one in his or her right mind could view these weapons themselves, and the complex that develops, manufactures, distributes, and then uses these weapons, as less likely to cause, rather than deter, war."

Here is a version of the second argument. It is one both pacifists and some nonpacifists could use. "Your argument so far is not very impressive, because you have failed to distinguish clearly between the two senses of 'deterrence.' In the first, more general sense, *any* weapon can, in theory, be used as a deterrent. In this sense, we can think of weapons as useful for good or bad purposes, which for the moment can be interpreted as meaning the same as useful for deterring or causing a needless war. By its very nature, any weapon can be used by a nation to help it carry out its expansionist policies. Conversely, any weapon can be displayed by a potential victim nation in the hope that it will frighten off the aggressor. In the second sense of 'deterrence,' in contrast, the deterrent functions of certain weapons are more pronounced than their nondeterrent functions. In this more specialized sense, some weapons possess certain features that make them more likely to be viewed as having the ability to prevent war. What you need in your argument against the pacifist assault is to point out not just why modern weapons deter wars in general, but why many of them do so more than others." At this point the two arguments combine.

What are the special features that make for deterrent weaponry? And are there enough of them around to make deterrent theories feasible in the foreseeable future?

So-called defensive weapons are the most obvious candidates as deterrent weapons. But what are defensive weapons? What specific features do weapons have to make them defensive? Although not one of the most successful weapons systems of all time, the Maginot Line was a paradigm of such a system. The line's main guns were placed in fixed bunkers and could be used only when France was under attack. Another not so successful defensive system was found in Singapore during World War II. The coastal artillery used to defend this city faced out to sea and was thus useless when the Japanese attacked from land. In addition to guns and military personnel found in fixed bunkers, coastal artillery, and fortresses, other paradigmatic examples of defensive weaponry include radar whose main purpose is to identify and help destroy incoming attack airplanes and missiles, short-range (interceptor) fighter planes, antiaircraft weaponry ranged around cities and other possible targets, coastal submarines, various small short-range or

patrol-type surface naval craft, land and sea mines, and, as we have
seen, surveillance satellites. From this list it appears that most defensive
weapons can initially be characterized as having no more than a short
reach and thus at best can destroy enemy forces only when they come
within arm's length of these weapons. Many of these weapons also
appear to have a certain passive character to them, so they cannot be
altogether appealing to the likes of Generals Patton and Rommel, but
also to most military leaders. More on this point shortly.

Another way of specifying the features of at least some defensive
weapons is in terms of the objects they are designed to destroy. If the
main function of an interceptor, such as the Soviet Mig-25, is to destroy
strategic bombers (who by definition are designed to strike deep in
enemy territory), then it can be called defensive (Dunnigan 1983, 352–
53). An endo-atmospheric (that is, within the atmosphere) antimissile
missile would similarly be defensive in nature. Antitank weapons are
also mainly defensive because tanks themselves are ideal offensive
weapons, combining as they do great destructive power, the ability to
reach out behind enemy lines, and a fair amount of speed.

This contrast between defensive weapons and their targets suggests
that a better understanding of the former leads to a better understanding
of the latter (that is, offensive weapons). Would, for example, the U.S.
B-2 qualify as an offensive weapon (*Jane's Defence Weekly*, December 3,
1988, 1376–77; Sweetman 1988b, 1377)? It would seem so because it is a
strategic bomber, even though it achieves its goal of defending itself as
it penetrates enemy territory by utilizing electronic and other stealth
technology. Just because it thrives as a bomber by using various countermeasure technologies, it does not thereby become a defensive
weapon. These technologies, after all, are in place to enable it to attack
the enemy deep in its own territory.

Instead of using stealth, as the B-2 does, ICBMs penetrate enemy
territory and defend themselves by employing speed. These also are
classic offensive weapons, as are cruise missiles, tanks, personnel-
carrying fighting vehicles (such as the United States' Bradley and Soviet
Union's BMP), attack aircraft carriers, and long-range fighter bombers
(like the United States' F/A-18). Bridging equipment could also be added
to this list, although it might not be thought of as a weapon system as
such. Still, this equipment does belong here because offensive armies
need large quantities of such equipment to repair the bridges destroyed
by a nation defending itself against invasion. What seems to characterize
all these weapons as offensive is mainly that they help to carry the battle
to the enemy. Almost all have, relatively speaking, long reach—or in
the case of bridging equipment, it helps other weapon systems achieve

this long reach. In addition, the disabling function of these weapon systems is pronounced. Almost all of them have a big bang.

Basically, defensive weapons have a short reach (and, in the extreme, are passively fixed in place) and are often at their best in destroying offensive weapons. It might be supposed that another feature of defensive weaponry is invulnerability to attack. A mobile missile might in this sense be seen as an ideal defensive weapon because the enemy would have trouble destroying it in a war of aggression. But if this same mobile missile possesses intercontinental range and great accuracy, it would seem to qualify as a very good offensive weapon as well. Here again, as with the B-2, the notion of countermeasures should not be confused with that of a defensive weapon system. The mere fact that a missile's main countermeasure is movement (on the ground, at sea, or in the air) does not change the basic nature of the beast. If it has long reach, great accuracy, and destructive power, it is still basically an offensive weapon system. So merely having the feature of being difficult to attack hardly helps much in understanding what a defensive weapon is.

As they have been characterized thus far, defensive weapons do not seem especially commendable. Not many warriors would be happy fighting a war with just these weapons because it would likely be a losing war. Still, I have given a partial response to the second argument that the variety of deterrent weapons in this high-technology world is too limited to make a war-deterrent policy meaningful. Having surveillance satellites available hardly was enough to give much support to this policy. But now we see that a wide variety of modern weapons have defensive properties and thereby also possess special deterrent properties. So although the argument for adopting a deterrent war policy is apparently not terribly strong (because most defensive weapons are too passive to permit a nation relying on them to protect itself effectively), it at least is not totally ridiculous either.

Offensive Defense

In fact, the situation favoring deterrent policies is more favorable than I have thus far characterized it. Various writers have argued that in a major conventional war, modern technology favors defense over offense (Hannig 1981, 1439–43; Barnaby 1984c, 79–80). The reason is not hard to see. Some of the most impressive developments in modern weaponry have occurred with antitank weaponry, for example. To be sure, over time tanks have proved more resistant to attack than many would have supposed. Most recently tanks have come to be protected with reactive armor, which reacts to a hit on a tank by causing small surface explosions, thereby mitigating the destructive effects of the missile explosion. Still, even with these defensive improvements, modern antitank weaponry is getting smarter and shows promise of making mass tank attacks very costly. The United States' TOW missile, developed in the 1960s, is relatively smart but is not particularly effective in tracking enemy armor in a war environment of smoke, fog, and dust. Newer versions (for example, the TOW 2A) make this weapon system more effective in this regard. Still, in the future, there is promise of greater smartness and lethality in dealing with modern tanks. Various technologies are being considered, among them being hypervelocity kinetic missiles (which do not explode but merely ram the tank) and various "fire and forget" missiles (which can reach a target on their own after being launched) (U.S. Army 1988, 392). Other weapons, such as Maverick, have been developed or are being developed to attack tanks from the air (Lambeth 1987, 97). So-called millimeter-wave technology is in the offing (Barnaby 1984c, 76). This technology promises to make these defensive weapons even more immune to the smoke and dust of battle and even less susceptible to countermeasures than the weapon systems available today. All this smartness in antitank weaponry may not render the tank obsolete, but it will make it extremely costly for an attacking army to use them in large numbers to spearhead an attack. This is so because antitank weapons, costing tens of thousands of dollars apiece, will probably be able to consistently destroy tanks costing in some cases well over a million dollars each.

Of course this same smartness built into antitank weapons can be used to make air assaults costly as well. Attackers will be faced with a variety of locating and reaching weapons to make helicopter and airplane sorties over a well-defended area expensive. Other technologies can also be used to make an attack costly. Countless numbers of plastic (and smart) mines can be quickly laid to extract still more costs from an attacking enemy, both in men and material. Further, modern communications aided by remotely piloted vehicles will make it possible for the defender to monitor the direction of an attack in ways not possible in the past. After all, attackers cannot help but be out in the open more than defenders, so such technology will tend to favor the defenders to some extent at least.

Taken together, modern weapons technology may well be playing more of a deterrent than a war-causing role. This seems to be true at least with respect to those war-threatening settings where technology is most fully developed.

However, a complication in this optimistic picture requires examination. Thus far, our picture of defensive fighting (and by inference of deterrent policies) has made it look disturbingly passive. Even with all the fancy modern defensive equipment used to its full potential, it might be supposed that the offense would still have many advantages. After all, even if a defensive army reacts quickly to an attack, it is still reacting. It is not choosing when and where to fight the battle. It might seem therefore that always being one step behind would put the defender at a disadvantage. Those who might be most distressed by this reactive or relatively passive posture of the defender have often expressed themselves by saying: "The best defense is a good offense."

This dramatizes the complication alluded to above. If the defense is going to get offensive, how will it be possible to make a distinction between defensive (and therefore deterrent) from offensive (and therefore nondeterrent) postures of military forces? It will help to make a distinction between fighting an aggressive war and fighting a war aggressively. The former pertains to how wars get started, that is, to the justice or injustice of the war. *Aggressor* expresses a negative verdict that the war has been started unjustly. In contrast, fighting a war aggressively pertains to the war itself. In this sense, there is no contradiction in saying that an army in a defensive posture waiting for a war to start can fight aggressively once that war starts.

However, to fight aggressively inevitably involves investing in weapons other than short-range interceptors, antitank guns, coastal submarines, and the like. At a minimum, such a strategy generates a need for long-range fighter bombers that can intercept and destroy not just the enemy forces immediately engaged in battle but also their follow-on forces. These large and mobile follow-on forces, waiting to attack when openings in the victim nation's defenses have been found, have a good chance of overwhelming even the most effective passive defenses facing them. It therefore would seem advisable for any wise defense to take on these follow-on forces before they are deployed in battle. The strategy here would be to strike these forces to destroy as many of them as possible or at least to confuse and disorganize them enough so that they would be ineffective even if deployed. Achieving this would require not only fighter bombers but also attack and troop-carrying helicopters. Various smart weapons, including missiles armed with a variety of submunitions to stop the aggressor, would also need to be deployed. It is almost as if, once the battle begins, it would be difficult to tell from the way the two sides deploy their forces which one was fighting a war of aggression and which was not.

In fact, it would still be possible to tell them apart. The aggressor nation would likely require more tanks and other armored vehicles compared to the nonaggressor. The aggressor would likely have more personnel committed to battle (assuming no great technological discrepancy exists between the two enemies) simply because attack requires larger forces to get the job done than does defense. Although the two antagonists would look more alike than one might at first suppose, when the totality of their weaponry is taken into account, differences should be apparent. An aggressive defender would look and act differently from an aggressive aggressor.

The implication of this point is that before the war begins, it should be possible to distinguish between two well-armed nations as to who is the potential aggressor and who is the potential victim. Or, putting it differently, it should be possible to distinguish between a nation in a war-of-aggression posture from one well-armed but in a deterrent posture. It is not as if, as some pacifist would have it, the only way to distinguish the aggressor from the nonaggressor is in terms of who is armed and who is not.

More Confusion of Offense and Defense

It was admitted earlier that any weapon could be thought of as a deterrent and, in that sense, be thought of as a defensive weapon. Even nuclear-armed ICBMs capable of starting and ending a war could be claimed by their owner to be in place "for defensive" or "for deterrent" purposes. Of course, that poses a problem for the nation targeted with these weapons. The same problem is posed with strategic bombers, long-range cruise missiles, attack carriers capable of taking the war to any nation's heartland, and other long-reach weapons. The potential target of these weapons cannot discern their purpose because these weapons are ambiguous.

The difficult question requiring an answer here is whether these weapons need to be deployed even if we assume the purity of the defensive nation's intentions. The related question is, what are the dangers of such deployments? These questions will be discussed in the next chapter. A discussion of the deterrent role of nuclear weapons will follow the chapter after that one.

CHAPTER FIVE

Strategic Weapons

Introduction

The argument in the previous chapter says it is misleading to morally condemn modern weaponry carte blanche because a wide variety of modern weapons are not inherently provocative. Quite the contrary, weapons production and deployment characterized as defensive or, at least nonoffensive, apparently are more likely to deter rather than cause war. Far from having a moral duty not to have these weapons, we can make a case for having a duty to go the other way. Nations under threat of war would be immoral if they did not possess these weapons because, by not having them, they would be encouraging war and all the suffering associated with it.

But even if these arguments are correct, there is a question about possessing offensive weapons—in particular, strategic offensive weapons. After all, these weapons receive the most attention from those who argue for the immorality of modern weaponry, and with good reason. If, for purposes of deterrence, nations felt it necessary to possess ICBMs and long-range bombers, as well as tactical offensive weapons such as hordes of tanks, helicopters, mobile artillery, and mechanized personnel carriers, then it no longer would be so easy to distinguish peace-loving nations from potential aggressors. That being the case, none of the nations involved in maintaining such weapons could possibly live in relative comfort and relaxation behind a shield created by their defensive-minded military. Instead, they would be in an environment of suspicion and arms escalation. Focusing on just such an environment, we can see how the arguments from the previous chapter have not blunted the thrust of the big argument. Instead, now more than before, we can also see how an important part of the big argument's message is that offensive weapons are the real villains of the peace.

Is it, then, morally permissible or even necessary for potential-victim nations to have strategic and other offensive weapons in their arsenals? The suggestion so far has been that it would be nice if they did not because the doctrine of deterrence would then be more clearly distinguishable from that of aggression. But quite apart from how nice it might be, is it necessary?

Options

First, it is important to lay out the options available to nations with respect to these weapons. One option is to design, build, and deploy a wide variety of offensive weapons. In practice as well as theory, these weapons could be tactical, strategic, or both. However, because the following discussion will focus mostly on strategic offensive weapons, this will be called the strategic option. At the other extreme, nations could opt not to design, build, and deploy any of these weapons. This will be called the nonstrategic option. There are some in-between options as well. One is to design offensive weapons but not build or deploy them. Another is to design, build, and deploy weapons that fall through the cracks. The Soviet Backfire bomber, for example, is not a true strategic weapon, but it could be used for this purpose in a pinch. Still another option is to design, build, and deploy some, but not the full range of, strategic weapons. Finally, a nation could choose to deploy only a certain (smaller or larger) number of these weapons.

There are also the negotiation and the nonnegotiation options. These options are a matter of degree because two or more nations could decide to negotiate away the existence of a few, many, or all their strategic weapons. Or, less dramatically, they could negotiate to regulate a few, many, or all their strategic weapons, and they could do this regulating with respect to one or more features of their weapons.

Other options available have a kind of backup or secondary status. Even though nations might not be negotiating over anything, they could still establish hot lines and other lines of communication to minimize the chance of misunderstanding leading to war. Or, as the United States and the USSR have done with their bombers (the B-1 and the Blackjack, respectively), they could allow civilian and military representatives from the other side to look over their new weapons. Presumably this openness has the same salutary effect as surveillance satellites have of preventing surprise. Along these same lines, the two nations might invite each other to various meetings and conferences, or even to military exercises. They could also encourage educational, cultural, and other exchange programs. Imagination might suggest other possibilities.

Two things should be noted about these backup options. One is that they do not exclude some of the primary options. Two nations could engage in negotiations and at the same time engage in cultural exchanges. The second is that most of these secondary options are "apple pie." They represent unalloyed good for most people.

The Negotiation Option

Most people would say the same thing about the negotiation option. It seems so intuitively sensible when contrasted to the strategic option that the latter can easily be made to look both stupid and immoral. "Why not," defenders of this option ask, "negotiate most, or better yet all, of these strategic weapons away? If we do, then all we would need are defensive weapons. With only such weapons in hand, money wasted for expensive military hardware and training could be used to solve health, poverty, and environmental problems; and wars would be less likely. Further, once the strategic weapons are abolished, people would come to wonder why they need all their defensive weapons. After all, many defensive weapons are in place because of a proliferation of offensive weapons. So with the elimination of offensive weapons, many defensive weapons would also be eliminated. When this happens, even more money would be saved and still more help would be forthcoming for dealing with our social problems."

This argument, a variant of the big argument, has a certain force. Not only does it highlight the "villainous" role of offensive weapons, but it reminds us that buying such weapons is a waste. Money spent on these weapons could be put to better use.

Still, in the form presented, the argument misleads us to some extent. The negotiation option is not directly opposed to the strategic option, but to the nonnegotiation option. It is possible, therefore, to support both some variants of the negotiation and the strategic options. Thus, it is not contradictory to argue that strategic weapons should be deployed even if, in the end, some or all of them would be negotiated out of existence. To be sure, this is an extremely expensive way to accomplish the end of getting rid of these weapons. Nonetheless, that seems to be what happened when the United States deployed its Pershing II and land-based cruise missiles in Europe, before negotiating them out of existence. The argument in favor of this expensive diplomatic maneuver is that the Soviets would not have given up their already-in-place SS-20 missiles if the Pershings and the cruise missiles were not already deployed. "Why," the Soviets probably asked themselves, "should we give up real missiles in exchange for ones existing only on paper?"

So it is more than a remote theoretical possibility to support both the negotiation and the strategic options. Still, this is not to say that this combination of options is the most morally acceptable. Strong defenders of the big argument would counter by reminding us of the dangers of deploying strategic weapons. Indeed, they too can cite a classic case, the cruise missile, to support their argument. "Admittedly," they will argue, "land-based cruise missiles have been negotiated out of existence in Europe. But these missiles, both with nuclear and nonnuclear warheads, have also been deployed in all sorts of naval vessels and aircraft. Perhaps even these missiles can be negotiated out of existence in the near future. But this will not be easy because these weapons are small and thus easy to move about and hide. But what one must remember is that the United States developed these missiles originally as so-called bargaining chips in exchange for some concession on the USSR's part. But after seeing their potential, the United States became enamored with them, and now both sides have them. Thus, what was to be a bargaining chip to help make the threat of other strategic weapons diminish, has itself turned into a new and dangerous strategic weapon. What do you strategic option people want? More new bargaining chips so you can negotiate away the old ones like the cruise?"

These arguments for combining the negotiation and strategic options, on the one side, and for choosing the former while rejecting the latter, on the other, help explain why the negotiation option by itself has such a favorable image. So far, everybody in the debate favors this option. The difference between the two sides is not about the ends to be sought but the means for getting to those ends. Those favoring what might be called the dual-option approach take the hard line of negotiating through strength, while the nondeployers take a softer line. Only a few truly hard-liners would oppose any version of the negotiation option; very likely, some of them would oppose this option not in principle but because they fear, on the one side, it might lead to premature euphoria and a "lowering of one's guard" and, on the other, to treaty cheating.

Arguments for Deploying Strategic Weapons

But who is right here? If the question is simply, should a nation temporarily adopt the strategic option as a step toward negotiating its strategic weapons away? then probably neither side is. Negotiating without deploying certainly makes more sense when neither side has deployed, when the general climate between "enemies" is improving, or when the weapons being negotiated look particularly menacing. Yet, if one side is perceived to be weak or the indications are that the "enemy" is intransigent, then the dual-options approach might make more sense. Neither approach will likely work in all contexts, and neither one can be taken without risks.

But what of the two questions raised earlier? Should a nation deploy strategic weapons to be in a better position to negotiate? And should potential-victim nations arm themselves with strategic weapons in the first place? Putting themselves in a better position to negotiate might be one reason why they should, but what other reasons might there be?

One powerful reason is related to the rapid changes taking place in military development. It was argued in chapter 4 that these changes now favor defense over offense insofar as conventional wars are concerned. But there is no guarantee that this trend will continue. It may do so indefinitely, in which case powerful aggressors will think twice, or several times over, before launching an aggressive war. It may even happen that, as this defensive technology spreads to the smaller nations, the advantage defense has over offense will act as a deterrent to war for them as well. But the trend may not continue and may not spread. New technology might reverse things so that even a nonaggressor nation might want to hedge its bets by having some strategic weapons available for deterrent purposes.

A related argument runs as follows. "It is only an untested theory that defense has the advantage over offense. There has not been a major war between two high-technology military forces since the high-technology revolution began two or three decades ago. We do not really know how well helicopters, modern tactical airplanes, tanks, and other offensive weapons will survive in a battle setting where electronics is used both to help destroy them and to help them survive. No doubt many weapons will disappoint their users. Others will please them. But given the fundamental nature of the changes taking place in weaponry, and the wide range of these changes across the whole weapons front, we cannot tell which will disappoint and which will please. That being the case, it would be foolish to bet the welfare of one's nation on a theory of the superiority of defense over offense. What is needed is perhaps a heavy investment in defensive weaponry, but also at least some investment in offensive weaponry as well. It is better to be safe than sorry. The paradox here is that peace itself has proved to be destabilizing. The fact that no major wars between high-technology nations have been fought for so long helps create this uncertainty, which, in turn, leads to more and more spending on weapons."

Here is another strong argument on behalf of those who would argue for the deterrent use of strategic weapons such as the United States' B-1 and B-2 bombers and the Soviet Blackjack bomber. Actually it is two arguments, but for the sake of convenience I will collapse them into one. It runs as follows. "Strategic weapons can do great damage to the enemy. If a nation is attacked by such weapons in such a way that it cannot respond in kind, it significantly increases its chances of losing that war (the main part of the first argument). Further, it is not easy to stop a strategic attack (the main part of the second argument). If the enemy attack is well prepared, some of its airplanes and missiles will inevitably get through even the best defenses. Once a war starts, to prevent aggressors from having a one-sided advantage, victim nations must be in position to respond in kind. But more important, having these weapons in hand will prevent war. Aggressor nations are more likely to attack when they see that they can do unto their victims what cannot be done unto them."

Another "cannot respond in kind" argument is worth mentioning. It was used after World War II, when it seemed that the Eastern bloc nations had an overwhelming advantage over the Western nations in conventional military forces (more men, tanks, artillery, etc.), while the West had an overwhelming advantage in strategic weaponry (more and better bombers). Even if it were assumed the West was never seriously interested in attacking the East, it was argued that it was necessary to maintain the strategic advantage to keep the East at bay. According to this argument, *strategic* weaponry might be needed to deter a potential enemy's overly abundant *tactical* forces.

I could present other arguments in favor of having even peace-loving nations maintain strategic weapons, but I will mention only one more, the vagueness argument. It is an argument touched on already in this study, but one that has not been discussed head-on as yet.

The vagueness argument begins by attempting to undermine the distinction between defensive and offensive weapons. It does so best by example. It asks, are the United States AEGIS cruisers defensive or offensive weapons? Because AEGIS represents systems of phased-array radar and fire-control equipment for defending ships at sea, the answer seems obvious: they are defensive. But what are they designed to defend? Themselves, to be sure. But ships like this are not put at sea to protect themselves. That would be stupid. Their purpose is to protect aircraft carriers. But aren't these carriers offensive weapons systems? Aren't they armed with long-range attack airplanes capable of carrying both conventional and nuclear weapons? Given that AEGIS cruisers defend offensive weapon systems, what are we to call them, defensive or offensive weapon systems?

Exactly the same point can be made about certain "Star Wars" weapon systems used to defend ICBMs. If the purpose of these defensive missiles is to help protect offensive weapon systems, how are they to be classified? Granted, these same missiles could be used to protect cities. But when they are used not for this purpose but for protecting missiles capable of reaching out six to seven thousand miles to destroy enemy targets, what are we to call them? The same question can also be asked of any other defensive weapon that can easily be, and often is, used to protect offensive weapons.

Having undermined the distinction between offensive and defensive weapons, those who advocate that even peace-loving nations deploy so-called strategic weapons will go on to express themselves as follows. "Weapons are weapons. If you permit the use of defensive weapons, you must also permit the use of offensive (strategic) weapons because there really is no difference between defensive and offensive weapons." Interestingly enough, pacifists might also be tempted by the vagueness argument insofar as it undermines the offensive-defensive weapons distinction. But, they would finish their argument differently. Although they too would insist that weapons are weapons, they would take this insight as a reason for abolishing the whole lot of them.

Assessing Options

The thrust of much of what I have been saying in the last two chapters suggests a lack of sympathy for this last argument. Weapons are not just weapons. To be sure, many weapons cannot be classified as either defensive or offensive, so there is a good deal of vagueness here. Yet it is possible to classify many either one way or the other. It is also possible, the argument states, to look at the mix of weapons to see whether a nation is in an offensive or defensive posture.

Nonetheless, the other arguments in the previous section suggest that even if defensive and offensive weapons can be distinguished, there is no bright line between the concepts "defensive" and "offensive" to identify which weapons potential victim nations should deploy and which they should not. In addition, there seem to be several good reasons for allowing these nations to deploy strategic weapons. But if there are, then the worst fears expressed in the big argument re-emerge. With both sides armed with quick-strike strategic weapons as well as with powerful, offensive tactical ones, war seems likely to occur—sooner or later—for any of the following reasons: paranoia on one side or the other caused by, for example, one side having a weapon or deploying it threateningly; errors in judgment, such as misreading radar data; accidental firing of a powerful weapon in the direction of the enemy; and calculations on one side that it has a winning window of opportunity.

The paradox is this: for a deterrent policy to be successful, strategic weapons need to be deployed. But if they are, deterrence seems to be put in jeopardy. The paradox is even more acute when the focus of attention shifts to the use of strategic nuclear weapons. The deterrent effect of these weapons seems to be great. People are especially afraid of starting wars when both sides possess these weapons. Yet deterrence seems compromised just because having these weapons invites errors, miscalculations, and even deliberate mischief that might lead to war of a kind so horrible as to defy the imagination. How is the paradox to be resolved? I turn to this question in the next chapter.

· CHAPTER SIX ·

Nuclear Weapons

Introduction

This talk about a paradox is still another way of stating a portion of the big argument (Cohen and Lee 1986, 9–13; McMahan 1989, 407–10). In terms of the paradox, this portion can be restated as follows. Even if the fright associated with possessing nuclear weapons has a war-deterring effect, possessing such weapons has other effects (for example, nervousness, tensions) that undermine deterrence. More than that, this undermining is so extensive as to make the deterrent thesis broken-backed (Donaldson 1985, 537–48). Accordingly, the overwhelming and quite legitimate fright we feel about nations possessing these weapons should not lead to the choice of the strategic option, but to its opposite.

Part of this argument's force stems from the assumption that these weapons are so destructive as to make any legitimate use of them impossible. For weapons to be weapons, it is also assumed, they must have some military use. In principle, nuclear weapons must be able to help one side win a war over the other, or at least serve some war purpose, such as stopping an enemy attack in a way that allows the defender to survive. However, because the use of nuclear weapons leads to the destruction of all the participants in war, they cannot be weapons by definition.

But even if this (partial) definition of a weapon is accepted, it is not clear that nuclear weapons satisfy it. Certainly they count as weapons when only one nation has them, for they can then be used to destroy the military power of the nonpossessing nation. To be sure, in most settings this would be an immoral use of these weapons. Yet consider the following scenario, where both sides are armed to the teeth with nuclear weapons and, at the same time, it is not obvious their use is morally illegitimate. Country A initiates a war by attacking country B's military installations and population centers with nuclear weapons. We can assume this attack is clearly immoral. The attack is of such a force that B is no longer a viable nation economically, politically, or socially. It has been defeated. However, because B has maintained many nuclear warheads and a wide variety of systems to deliver them, it is still capable of retaliation. In fact, it does retaliate but does so by using its most sophisticated nuclear weapons to destroy country A. B's counterattack kills several hundred thousand civilians in A, but this is nowhere near the number killed by A. Because country B's attack focuses on military and selected governmental targets (leaving enough of the latter so there is someone with whom to negotiate), it effectively destroys A so it cannot profit from its aggressive first-strike attack (Art 1985, 510). In responding not quite in kind, B has adopted neither a war-winning (nor even a defensive) strategy, but one best described as war crippling.

This is an important distinction. When it is not made, one is tempted to argue that if a nation cannot use nuclear weapons to win a war or simply to defend itself, because their use would precipitate mutual destruction, these weapons cannot have any use in war at all. But the argument here is that such weapons can have a use as war cripplers. Beyond that, I am arguing, this use may well be morally permissible.

How can this be, when using these weapons will lead predictably to killing many civilians? In addition, how can this be, because unleashing a retaliatory attack may increase the chances of a worldwide environmental breakdown in the form of radiation, smoke, pollution, and other side effects of the attack itself?

Dealing with the second question first, I suggest that a counterstrike could be the straw to break the environment's back, but this is not necessarily so. It is a distinct possibility that although such a strike will further damage the environment, the damage will not override the good reasons for striking back in the first place. Given the increasing capabilities of modern weapons to locate and reach an enemy, and to accomplish these tasks with great precision, this possibility will become more likely in the future. With newer and more precise weapons in hand, the bang required to cripple a nation will not have to be so large as it would have been twenty, or even ten, years ago.

Notice how the scenario can be modified to take account of the environment. Imagine that country B initially and reflexively strikes back at A in a limited way only. Minutes after the original attack, B's nuclear weapons destroy a few of the most important and vulnerable enemy military and governmental targets—especially those that might be used to further damage B or destroy other nations. Rather than unleashing all it has at its command, B holds back many of its counter-strike weapons to assess the situation. Let us say it can do this because it has a large number of invulnerable nuclear submarines armed with very accurate ballistics (like the U.S. second-generation D-5 Trident) and cruise missiles. After reflecting on what it should do, B determines that selective but destructive strikes will cripple the enemy without signifi-cantly destroying the environment for the rest of mankind. Let us assume B can unleash its destruction in such a way as to cripple A to the point where it will lose rather than gain power. A's aggression will leave it weaker rather than stronger. Thus, by counterstriking in the way it has, B will have saved the rest of the world from being dominated by a nation cruel enough to have started (no doubt foolishly) the most immoral war ever conceived.

But what about the first question above? What of the innocent civilians in A who would die as the result of B's so-called limited counterstrike? In a way, the same reply also applies to this question. Whatever number would have died if a comparable attack had taken place a generation ago, or even if it were to take place today, many fewer would need to die in a future war. The smaller but more accurate weapons of tomorrow will simply have fewer side effects compared to the massive nuclear weapons of today and yesterday—provided they are committed to battle discriminatingly. In short, a policy of retaliation makes more sense militarily and morally today than it did in the past, and such a policy will make still more sense in the future.

One might object that even when responding with care, B has violated the discrimination principle. Held to strictly, this principle forbids any nuclear response. Even the most accurate nuclear weapons cannot be anything but immoral because, the objection continues, there are too many military targets located too close to too many population centers to draw any other conclusion. Any kind of nuclear attack, careful or not, cannot help but kill more than an acceptable number of civilians and, therefore, cannot help but violate the principle.

But has the discrimination principle been violated? Certainly it has been, if it is interpreted in such terms that any battle will automatically be labeled immoral when civilian casualties reach a level of, say, 100, 1,000, or 10,000. However, consider the following. Even a small battle may violate the principle if it could have been predicted with some assurance that 50 or so civilians will die in the process of disabling one enemy sniper. Yet a larger battle may not be violating the principle, even though 1,000 civilians die, if the good coming from it is large enough. Citing civilian casualties strictly "by the numbers" simply makes no sense here. One has to assess whether there has been a violation of this principle by taking account of the context. If a battle has worldwide implications, it may still make sense to argue for not having violated the discrimination principle, even though many thousands of civilians will die.

My reply may seem as if it represents just another example of how utilitarian, cost-benefit thinking encourages us to slide gradually into an abyss of evil. However, this reaction misses the point of the reply. Not even ethical theorists who eschew utilitarianism and talk instead of duties or rights can avoid facing certain basic conflicts. Duties and rights themselves cannot help but generate conflicts sooner or later. So if, for example, the discrimination principle is stated in terms of a duty to refrain from killing innocent civilians, it does not follow that we must carry out this duty in all circumstances. We might have another duty— to protect certain people, for example—that cannot be carried out without leading to the death of many innocent people. In these circumstances, one duty overrides another. So it is not obvious on any account, utilitarian or otherwise, that country B's counterattack with nuclear weapons violates the discrimination principle and thereby is immoral. It might be immoral if it were to be carried out prematurely or carelessly. And even if these faults were avoided, it might also be judged immoral later (when looked back at historically) because of some miscalculations. Still, B's retaliation might not have been a mistake and might not have been a violation of the discrimination principle.

Another objection to the idea of moral uses of nuclear weapons runs as follows. "Looked at narrowly, using nuclear weapons in certain restricted settings may make some sense. However, looked at more broadly, a retaliatory policy like the one portrayed above undermines the deterrent thesis of Mutual Assured Destruction (MAD) by tempting nations to start taking war-winning policies seriously once again. If nations build these very accurate weapons, might they not come to think they can decapitate the enemy and thereby win a war by striking first? After all, if country B has these weapons, what is to prevent A from also having and using them for its evil purposes?"

Nothing, of course. But what follows from admitting that both nations have the capability of making accurate strikes at each other? Certainly not that war-winning policies will become fashionable again. What follows instead is Mutual Assured Destruction on a more sophisticated plane. In the future, as weapons become more refined, MAD will come to mean something less than the total destruction of a society. Total destruction will always represent one form of MAD. But another lesser form will be possible, one where a society's governmental, military, and scientific institutions can be devastated. This lesser form of MAD will still represent a form of this position because in the end whatever nation strikes first will suffer irreparable or long-term destruction of its major institutions. Far from being in a position to dominate the world, the aggressor nation instead will find itself so crippled that it is liable to military and economic domination by one or more of the bystander nations.

Nuclear Deterrence

Let us see where we stand. In part, the scenario of countries A and B is designed to show that it is not a contradiction to talk of the moral use of nuclear weapons. If there were a contradiction, it would be difficult to justify having these weapons in hand even for deterrent purposes (Goodin 1985, 641–58). For example, one could ask how it is possible to justify threatening a nuclear counter strike if every use of these weapons is immoral. However, because some moral uses of these weapons can be conceived, possessing these weapons is not an automatic sign of immorality. Therefore, a nation desiring to be on the side of the angels when war is threatening (that is, to be a nonaggressor) is justified in having these weapons in the first place. Further, by having these weapons and by being willing to use them, a nation need not worry about the credibility of its deterrent. Any nation contemplating aggression against such an angelic nation would have to take the latter's deterrent posture more seriously than if it knew the angel were a follower of the big argument. For deterrent purposes, of course, the nonaggressor nation need not make it clear in every possible scenario when it would actually use nuclear weapons. What if A restricted its initial act of aggression to counterforce (that is, military and semimilitary) targets? Would B respond in kind? What if the attack were limited to a few counterforce targets where A's intent was not to destroy B, but merely to shock it into submission? Or what if A did not use nuclear weapons but initiated a war of aggression with conventional weapons only, and carried it forth to the point where B was about to be decisively defeated? Would B respond by using a few or many nuclear weapons in any of these scenarios? By not making it clear what it would do in these and other similar situations, B makes its deterrent policies even more credible.

Still, having shown that deterrence can be a morally credible policy is not the same as showing it to be the most credible policy available. At most, the arguments in this chapter prevent those sympathetic with the big argument from winning a cheap victory over the defenders of the strategic option. Thus, the defenders of the big argument can still argue that although using nuclear weapons is morally acceptable *in theory*, it is not acceptable *in practice*, because the reasons favoring nonuse always override those for use in the final analysis.

When the issue between the defenders of the big argument and the defenders of the strategic option is put in this form, it is difficult to know what to say (Hardin and Mearsheimer 1985, 411–23). It is as if the serious and complex nature of the problems associated with possessing nuclear weapons overwhelm the logic and the facts to which we appeal in dealing with them (Goodin 1985, 642–45). Still, it is appropriate to make certain comments and recommendations that in the end will lean somewhat in the direction of the strategic option. What I have to say falls under six general headings: (1) the difficulties in getting rid of nuclear weapons; (2) the problem of deciding who should have these weapons; (3) the question of what kinds of nuclear weapons should be retained; (4) the issue of quantity versus quality with respect to these weapons; (5) the question of defense against nuclear attack; and, finally, (6) the big argument's impact on the position I am arguing for concerning nuclear weapons.

First, it is difficult to imagine a world totally devoid of nuclear weapons. Agreements, even if they contained enforcement provisions, would be difficult to enforce. The difficulty is not just with eliminating the weapons held by today's major nuclear powers, but also with other nations that either have nuclear weapons in small numbers or will likely have them soon (Barnaby 1984a, 44–56). As everyone knows, nuclear weapons proliferation is a serious problem. Further, even if all weapons were destroyed at any one point in time, it might be difficult to keep certain nations from building new ones. Plus, agreement is one thing; actually destroying all these weapons is quite another. If all nations agreed to destroy all their nuclear weapons, it would be the supreme surprise to discover that one or two nations were cheaters and had somehow managed to squirrel away a dozen or so bombs. The political effect of the supreme surprise would be devastating.

Second, if these weapons cannot be disinvented, we must live with the idea that at least some nations will possess them. A few nations might opt out by practicing unilateral disarmament, but others would

not. Unilateral disarmament would be easiest for smaller nations operating under someone else's nuclear umbrella because there would then
be no major shift in the balance of power among nations. In contrast,
the political (and moral) consequences would be much more serious if a
major nuclear power opted out. These consequences would affect the
so-called liberal democracies most directly because it is more likely that
they would be the ones to take the unilateral plunge.

It does not require much imagination to determine the effects on
these nations that unilaterally disarm. They would experience some
economic benefit by not spending money on nuclear weapons, and they
would be less likely to be attacked with nuclear weapons because the
nations still possessing these weapons might not feel the need to use
them. However, those nations still with nuclear weapons might use
them to show the have-nots they meant to dominate them. But the
chances are they would not use these weapons, because they could get
what they wanted simply by threatening to do so. So the haves could
dictate all sorts of political and economic conditions and in short order
make the have-nots their clients. The power over the have-nots would
likely extend indefinitely because once the haves become dominant,
they could prevent the have-nots from ever becoming haves again. The
net result could be the demise of the have-nots as independent states.
(For a contrary view, see Naess 1986, 427.) Once they lost their indepen-
dence, the nagging question facing the have-nots would be whether the
loss was all for nothing. What if the war that was prevented never would
have taken place in the first place?

Third, if some nations must possess nuclear weapons, decisions
have to be made about the kinds and numbers of weapons they should
keep in their arsenals. Should they be tactical or strategic weapons, or
both? Of these two classes, the former seem more benign (if that is the
right word) because many weapons falling in this class are defensive in
nature. As such, these weapons would have the advantage of not
frightening potential enemies as much as certain strategic weapons
would. Still, one needs to ask why a nation would want to have a large
array of tactical nuclear weapons in the form of mines, artillery shells,
warheads (on short-range rockets), and bombs (on tactical attack aircraft). Is the intent to actually develop a nuclear war-fighting capability?
That would seem insane if potential enemies also possessed a large
number of these weapons. The obvious danger of a war-fighting policy
with nuclear weapons would be escalation. In the confusion of a war
fought hundreds of miles on both sides of the front edge of the battle
area, it would not be easy to tell the difference between tactical and
strategic weapons, even assuming the antagonists wanted to distinguish

between the two. The nuclear war would spread far beyond the battle
area's front edge so that mutual destruction would literally take place
everywhere.

In addition, there is the "use them or lose them" problem with
certain tactical weapons, in particular land mines and short-range artillery. Deployed close to the battle area's front edge, these weapons could
easily be lost to the enemy. A modern fluidlike war encourages such
losses on both sides. It might therefore be tempting to use these
weapons so they would not be lost, even though the war had been
fought with conventional weapons up to that point.

Thus far, the dangers in using these weapons are all on the side of
those who would defend the big argument. However, one scenario
suggests a reason for deploying at least some of these weapons even if
they have many disadvantages. That reason is related to what Walzer
calls a supreme emergency (1977, 251–68; 1988, 6–21). If a nation were
to face total annihilation or utter defeat at the hands of a nation
practicing genocide, a case might be made for using tactical nuclear
weapons to head off that defeat—even on a first-use basis. Or the victim
nation might be justified in simply threatening the use of such weapons
to deter defeat.

If these are the primary scenarios for legitimate uses or threatened
uses of tactical nuclear weapons, there would be no need for any nation
to possess vast quantities of them. Vast quantities suggest the military
and political leaders of a nation are holding onto a war-winning strategy. The policy advocated here falls short of such a strategy even though
it goes beyond being abolitionist. It is best labeled a war-ending or war-
crippling strategy. The numbers of tactical nuclear weapons required to
implement such a strategy would perhaps be in the hundreds, but not
in the thousands. As to the types of such weapons, they would best be
mounted on missiles well back of the battle area's front edge so they
would not have to be committed to battle for fear of being lost. Or they
would be carried by aircraft based well back of the main battle area.
This, indeed, is the policy NATO has been following for some time.

Fourth, as with tactical nuclear weapons, quality is more important
for strategic weapons than quantity. If, as has been suggested already,
these weapons should be used only in a counterforce mode, they would
need to be extremely accurate. To be sure, not all counterforce strikes
require the highest degree of accuracy. Airfields, naval bases, army
bases, and many military manufacturing facilities are large enough to
make it possible for many present-day missiles to hit them with relative
ease. But there are certainly other military targets, such as missile silos
(those still loaded after the first strike), command headquarters, and

communications facilities, that would challenge missile and warhead technology to the utmost. Nonetheless, weapons capable of hitting these kinds of targets are required for maintaining a credible nuclear deterrent. No doubt, this means that expenditures on these weapons should not be diminished significantly in the future. They may, in fact, have to increase. New weapons, such as the United States' D-5 submarine-launched missile and the Soviet Union's SS-24 and SS-25 land-based missiles, need to be developed and deployed. Perhaps even more accurate missiles need to be developed on both sides. Complementing this construction would be the systematic destruction of large numbers of less accurate missiles. Presumably this would best be done through bilateral or multilateral agreements.

Fifth, in addition to being accurate, the arsenal of strategic nuclear weapons should be relatively invulnerable to attack (Bertram 1988, 311–12). Having even the most accurate nuclear weapons sited in a way that makes them vulnerable to a first-strike attack serves no deterrent purpose. Quite the contrary, such a tempting siting might invite an attack. So submarine-based and movable land-based missiles are to be preferred over fixed, land-based ones.

Strategic Defense against Nuclear Attack

There is another possibility here. Fixed-in-place missiles could be made invulnerable if they were protected. Basically this protection could be brought about in one (or both) of two ways. Either these missiles could be "hardened" (that is, placed in silos resistant to all but direct hits), or they could be protected by other defensive missiles. Neither option ought to be rejected out of hand. The former option already exists. Both the Soviet Union and the United States have spent much treasure to harden their missile sites. Although such hardening does not guarantee the survival of these missiles, it does protect them long enough so that a potential attacker would have to be concerned about a significant counterstrike from those missiles not hit directly during the initial assault.

The latter option is not a reality as yet, and may never be. The technology of defending missiles against attack from either ballistic or cruise missiles is in its infancy. Further, the moral issues surrounding the deployment and use of these weapon systems are complex (Kavka 1985, 673–91; Biddle 1987, 26–30, 32–35, 38; Schefter 1988, 46–50, 110, 112). This much should be clear, however. It would not be necessary to deploy a full-bodied defensive system to protect fixed missile silos. Nor would a complete defensive system be required to defend other military targets, such as airfields where a nation's strategic bombers are based. What is needed is a defensive shield strong enough to allow a nation's counterforce systems an opportunity to survive an initial attack. Even if an airfield was later destroyed because its defensive shield was eventually overwhelmed, the strategic bombers based on that field would have been given the opportunity by the shield to fly off elsewhere.

For these defensive purposes, only endo-atmospheric weapons would be required. Such defensive weapons operate within the atmosphere, whereas exo-atmospheric weapons operate in space. Opponents of defensive or antimissile systems focus most of their criticism against exo-atmospheric weapons. They point out quite rightly how terribly expensive these weapon systems would be. They also point out how these systems could be converted into quick-striking offensive weapons because many of their components would be sitting out in space—literally looking down at a potential enemy. Further, they would be vulnerable to counterattack because many of their components would be in fixed orbits. Finally, it is said, they would not be successful because the enemy could take countermeasures against them by, for example, launching missiles with quick-burn characteristics—thus making them more difficult to locate (*Jane's Defence Weekly*, July 16, 1988, 86–87). These and most other objections to defensive systems do not apply to endo-atmospheric defensive systems. These systems would simply be quick-firing, accurate missiles capable of picking off a high percentage of incoming attacking missiles. Their purpose in battle would be to gain time for the fixed-in-place missiles to enable them to survive long enough to be used in a counterstrike. In peacetime, their purpose would be to raise doubts in a potential enemy's mind about the likelihood of succeeding in a first-strike attack.

There are some objections to endo-atmospheric defensive systems as well. For one, they may not be cost-effective. The purpose of these missiles is to make a nation's counterstrike missiles invulnerable to attack, but that aim might be better accomplished by moving the latter missiles around on land, at sea (in submarines), or in the air. It remains to be seen whether this objection is legitimate. Research in defensive weaponry should decide the issue before the turn of the century.

But a second objection does not turn on how things might go technologically with these defensive systems. A variant of the vagueness argument discussed in the previous chapter, this argument says that some defensive weapons do not deserve to be called defensive, because they are in place to protect offensive weapons. In this case, the argument seems to have a good deal of bite to it because the endo-atmospheric missiles, as they are being talked about here, are in place to protect what many people consider the paradigm of an offensive weapon: ICBMs.

There is an obvious reply to this argument. The ICBMs being protected by the endo-atmospheric defensive system exist only to respond to acts of aggression. So although the defensive rockets are protecting offensive weapons, these weapons are not aggressive offensive weapons, only retaliatory ones.

This reply, however, fails to sense the main force of the argument against even the endo-atmospheric defensive weapons. That force can be best expressed by noting that an aggressor nation would also want these kinds of defensive weapons and have accurate ICBMs very much like those the victim nation would be interested in possessing. The aggressor nation would want the former because it would seek to protect its assets *after* it had launched its attack; and it would be interested in the latter because it would want its initial aggressive attack to be as effective as possible, especially against the victim nation's ICBM silos.

This powerful argument against endo-atmospheric defensive systems (as well as any other accurate and invulnerable nuclear weapon systems) is yet another variant of the big argument. It points out that what can be seen as a purely defensive system from the perspective of the nation possessing it will almost inevitably be seen as something sinister from the other side. The other side will ask: "Is the defensive system in place to reintroduce some sort of war-winning strategy into modern warfare? With an effective defensive system, any nation armed with ICBMs could strike first and then wait for a counterstrike, which it could figure it could stop cold or at least blunt severely. In this sense, isn't a defensive system here really a highly destabilizing offensive system?

It would be if one side armed with nuclear weapons developed such a system (and perhaps an exo-atmospheric defensive system as well), but the other side did not. But this is not likely to happen. Deploying even an endo-atmospheric defensive system would be a highly public thing to do. All sorts of tests in near space would have to be made over a long time before the system could be deployed. Further, once the system neared the deployment stage, gigantic radar and missile-site facilities would have to be built. A nation concerned that these weapons would be used offensively would have ample warning about what might happen and could build a comparable defensive system to help deter its enemy's aggressive intentions. It could also develop various countermeasures (*Jane's Defence Weekly*, July 16, 1988, 86–87). Or it would have ample time to enter into negotiations to limit or eliminate these defensive systems.

Another argument against an endo-atmospheric defensive system is that it might be destabilizing if it were effective enough to fully or almost fully frustrate a counterattack to an initial act of nuclear aggression. This is hardly a serious objection, however, because such a system simply could not be that effective. If it could, planners would not be as concerned with developing exo-atmospheric defensive systems to complement their endo-atmospheric rockets and missiles. These exotic exo-atmospheric systems are supposed to be most effective because they would be designed to intercept the vast majority of missiles and warheads before they get well under way. Using both exo-atmospheric weapons (to destroy the attackers before they could deploy their many real and dummy warheads) and endo-atmospheric weapons (to destroy the warheads that have somehow evaded the exo-atmospheric system), an effective defensive system just might be possible. In contrast, the purpose of deploying just an endo-atmospheric defensive system is more humble. Such a system could not possibly be put in place as foolproof protection against a major first-strike nuclear attack. Its purpose would be to give a potential victim more time so that some of its more vulnerable military assets (ICBM silos, airfields, and civilian and military leaders) would have a chance to survive an initial attack. Given this extra time, a counterstrike could still be planned and launched.

Actually a minimal defensive system against ballistic missiles could have another purpose: besides delaying the negative effects of a massive nuclear attack, such a system could protect a nation against an isolated accidental attack or one inspired intentionally by a maverick nation or terrorist group possessing the capacity to mount only a limited attack. Deploying endo-atmospheric defensive missiles for this purpose would be expensive because each major city in a nation would need its own small family of defensive missiles, radar, and other facilities. Whether it would be cost-effective remains to be seen.

The generally favorable nature of these arguments toward a minimal missile defense system should not be misunderstood. I am not saying such a system should be built, nor am I saying that a more complex exo-atmospheric system should be built. Rather, I am trying to be open-minded about one possible way to make ICBMs and other counterstrike nuclear weapons resistant to a first-strike attack. In the end, it may be that the simpler, but still complex, expedient of moving these weapons around is the best way to get the job done. Developments in defensive weaponry against missiles, however, have been so impressive in the last decade or so that it would seem foolish not to explore this possibility further. Because these weapons might prove to be cost-effective, I believe the arguments on the other side are not strong enough to label these weapons immoral at least for now. The point here is that, in spite of certain objections, invulnerability is a desirable feature to have in a nation's nuclear strike force.

Now let's examine the last of the six general headings—namely, the extent to which the big argument has affected the position I am arguing for. Many things said in this chapter represent a rejection of what defenders of the big argument would say. Most of these defenders would certainly be opposed to spending more money to make ICBMs more accurate, and most would be opposed to any effort to deploy a defensive shield against attacks by nuclear missile attacks. Instead, they would talk about a freeze on all or most military spending or about radical and unilateral reductions in nuclear arsenals (Blake and Pole 1983, 1984).

Nonetheless, the big argument has had an effect on the position I am advocating. The dangers posed by nuclear weapons both in terms of their destructive power and their numbers have led to recommendations that the number and size of warheads be reduced. The accurate missiles spoken of favorably in this chapter generally carry smaller warheads. Historically, the monstrously large warheads found in the USSR's SS-18 and the United States' Titan missiles were used because these older missiles were not very accurate. What could not be achieved by accuracy was achieved more or less (mostly less) by a big bang. It is true that some people will raise the specter of war-winning policies when they hear talk of smaller warheads. They will argue that the masters of the military missiles will suppose a war can be won if the nuclear bang is whittled down to size. But the specter will exist only in their minds. As I have argued, smaller and very accurate missiles will still be devastating enough to assure mutual destruction. These weapons may not individually kill hundreds of thousands of people, but they will cause enough direct and indirect damage to make initiating a nuclear war grossly unprofitable. So although some of the recommendations presented here involve spending additional money for certain kinds of weapons, they nonetheless reflect many concerns expressed in the big argument.

The recommendations concerning the number of warheads that nations should hold also reflect many of these concerns. These recommendations, it will be recalled, include discarding older warheads so that the total number of missiles and warheads decreases significantly. Defenders of the big argument might wish for the destruction of all missiles and warheads, but I have argued that this is unrealistic. Still, to

the extent that significant reductions are recommended, the effects of
the big argument on my argument are evident.

Another effect of the big argument is the favorable attitude expressed here toward bilateral and multilateral negotiations. Again, most
defenders of the big argument prefer that more be done. Still, although
what has been said in this chapter is not in accord with what most
defenders of the big argument wish to see happen, overall, the power
of that argument has not failed to have its effects.

Chemical and Biological Weapons

Chemical Weapons—General Background

In some respects the ethical issues surrounding the use of chemical weapons in war are quite different from those of nuclear weapons. First, the former vary more than the latter in the effects they have on people and the surrounding environment (Krickus 1986, 420–22). In most forms, for example, so-called tear gases (CS, CN) are not lethal. They are used either as temporary disabling agents or as agents to harass enemy personnel and lower their fighting and operating efficiency. At the other extreme, nerve gases (GA or Tabun, GB or Soman, GP or CMPF, etc.) in certain concentrations are extremely deadly. Relatively small doses of these chemicals can kill humans and other animals within seconds by destroying their nervous system (Dunnigan 1983, 282–86). In between, there are chemicals, mostly in the form of gases, that blister the skin, injure the lungs, choke, suffocate, blind, and induce vomiting. In certain concentrations these chemicals are killers too. Even when they do not kill, however, they can cause immediate and long-term suffering. Then there are chemicals that can kill, but whose primary purpose is to affect the environment. The defoliant Agent Orange is the best known of these weapons.

A second way that chemicals and nuclear weapons differ is that an international protocol forbids the use of chemical weapons. The 1925 Geneva Protocol allows for the production, but not the use in war, of poisonous and asphyxiating gases (Thomas and Thomas 1970, 71–85;

Barnaby 1984d, 107). It is not completely clear what effects this protocol has had on how wars have been fought since 1925, but at least there is a tradition of law that can be cited to encourage nations not to use these weapons.

A third difference is that, in most forms, chemical weapons represent a lower level of technology. By combining chemicals available for various commercial purposes, nations can produce and stockpile poison gases with relative ease and low cost. This makes it difficult to know who has these weapons and in what quantity they possess them. In addition, use of chemical weapons is difficult to verify. Unlike nuclear weapons, these weapons do not announce themselves. Further, some dissipate quickly in the air. These features make chemical weapons "ideal" for small, out-of-the-way wars and also help explain why these weapons are sometimes viewed as the "atomic bomb of the poor" and less-developed nations (Braude 1988, 357). The fact that chemical weapons were used by the Egyptians in the Yemen Civil War during the 1960s, by the Iraqis in the Iran-Iraq war (Abramowitz 1987, 1063–69), by the Iraqis in their war against the Kurds (Bruce and Banks 1988, 715), and by the Cubans in the war against the UNITA forces in Angola (Braude 1988, 357) supports this view. There is also evidence that even a militarily more advanced country like Syria is prepared to use poison gas if it ever becomes entangled in another war with Israel (Abramowitz 1987, 1063–69).

In other respects, chemical weapons are like nuclear ones. Both are area weapons in two senses. First, they carry on their disabling function in the immediate area where they are deposited by guns, airplanes, rockets, or missiles. Second, both can disable living creatures when carried by winds to areas far beyond the immediate impact zone. With these characteristics, it is evident that poison gases are far more dangerous today than they were in World War I, if for no other reason than the increased reach of modern military technology. In World War I, reach was largely limited to the range possessed by artillery. In that war, gas tended to drift from trench to trench disabling mainly military personnel. In contrast, today's rockets and missiles can hit targets far behind enemy lines. If the target is an airfield, the drifting gas can quickly move into farm areas, villages, and towns, thereby also harming civilian populations. More than that, military forces now have the capability to use poison gases directly on these populations. Used in this way, chemical weapons can induce terror among refugees moving in large numbers and could thus help block enemy transportation and paralyze support installations (*Jane's Defence Weekly*, April 30, 1988, 652). In a war fought in Central Europe, the use of poison gas would have a devastating effect on hundreds of millions of people trying to move away from the battle.

Still another way these two weapons systems are alike is that they are militarily very effective. This is obvious with nuclear weapons; they have not been called the ultimate weapons for nothing. It is somewhat less obvious why chemical weapons are so effective. As noted already, they can kill and do so very quickly. Over and above that, however, they can do their nasty work before their victims know what has hit them because many of these gases are invisible and odorless. This makes them particularly effective in surprise attacks against military personnel who do not have equipment for detecting their presence and against civilians who would have little or no idea how to protect themselves.

Other gases are effective as military weapons even if the enemy detects their presence. In fact, these gases may be effective just because the enemy knows what is going on. The reason is that preventive measures against poison gases are very cumbersome. Gas masks and special clothing can be uncomfortable to wear especially in hot weather. Thus, an army wearing such equipment is not likely to be fighting at peak efficiency. Fatigue will set in quickly, and thus mistakes will be made. Those who use poison gas against such an army are likely to have an easy time of it. These gases affect the psychology of those attacked as well. It is demoralizing to see your buddies dying such horrible deaths and to wonder whether the silent killer has marked you as its next victim.

Because of their effectiveness, it is no wonder the temptation to use chemical weapons is so great. The temptation would be even greater if, as when dealing with guerrillas who operate in jungles (where poison gases are more persistent than in open areas), the enemy cannot respond in kind (Dunnigan 1983, 284). But the question relevant to this study concerns their justified use: Are there settings where it is not immoral to use poisonous gases?

Moral Uses of Chemical Weapons

Consider the following scenario. Two nations, A and B, are at war. Both are armed with chemical weapons of all kinds. At a crucial point during the war, nation A bolsters its offensive by using sarin (a nerve gas) and prussic acid (a so-called blood gas). Because of the element of surprise and because the gas use is extensive, A's offensive gains momentum. What should B do? Of course it should collect data about this use, and of course it should complain to whatever neutral governments might influence A to stop this violation of the 1925 Geneva Protocol. But time is precious. Further, there are no indications that A, seeing that its offensive is succeeding, is willing to bow to public opinion. In any case, public opinion has not yet mobilized, and by the time it might, A will have won its tainted victory. B thus needs to do something drastic or suffer defeat. Before all is lost, it counters A's poison gas offensive with a poison gas offensive of its own. A week or so later, A's offensive slowly grinds to a halt.

Many people would argue that B was not acting immorally by responding in kind. Indeed, B would not be acting *illegally*, because the 1925 Geneva Protocol evidently permits such responses (Thomas and Thomas 1970, 79). But as to the morality of B's response, many would argue for it even though B's use of poison gas caused suffering and death among many innocent civilians. They would also argue for it even though it might have caused excessive suffering among A's military personnel. No doubt, B's case would be helped if A in fact were the aggressor nation to begin with, and B, in using poison gases to stop A, did not do so in a totally indiscriminate fashion. If, finally, there were no other way to stop A from engaging in its immoral gas attacks than by responding in kind, few would argue that it acted immorally. B would not be expected to let its military forces be defeated and its people conquered by these attacks.

It makes little difference whether one considers this argument fundamentally utilitarian or not. A utilitarian argument would say that in the long run, more good than harm will come from countering A's action in kind than from simply suffering a defeat. Not only would aggression have been rewarded if B had not responded, but a precedent would have been set that wars can be won by using these nasty weapons. A nonutilitarian argument would say that B has a duty to its people to keep them from being conquered by a nation immoral enough to use poison gas. Or, the argument would say, A's citizens and the world in general have a right to be protected from such evildoers. However the details of the argument are developed, it is not obvious that when B responds in kind against A, it is responding immorally. Only theorists who hold to some absolute rule—such as that it is immoral to engage in any military activity where civilians will die or that the use of such immoral weapons as poison gas is always wrong (no matter what the circumstances)—would deny the plausibility of the above argument.

Although plausible, this argument does not necessarily show that what B did is morally correct. Thus if the argument is interpreted as basically a utilitarian one, B's leaders might have simply miscalculated. It can be imagined that rather than stopping A, what actually happened is that its counteruse of poison gases angered A into attacking B's civilian population with these weapons. The result, then, would have been escalation rather than de-escalation. However, if the original judgment to counterattack with poison gas was made on utilitarian grounds, this possibility should have been taken into account. Another possibility that should have been anticipated is that A's immediate response would be to escalate, but its long-term response would be to back off.

However B might have thought through the problem, there are no guarantees that it would not have made some gross miscalculation or misassessment. This is why the standard of conduct to which B should be held accountable is not certainty, but something less—such as that what it did was not obviously wrong.

The following is a more difficult scenario to deal with. Nation C attacks D's cities as well as its military forces with poison gas, causing many civilian casualties and also gaining military advantage. What should D do? Following the scenario with nations A and B, D would not be condemned if it responded by attacking C's military forces with poison gas. But the tougher question is whether it should respond in kind to C's attacks on its civilian population. Is it utilitarian to do so? Do not D's leaders have a duty to their own people to do so and, paradoxically, a duty to C's innocent civilians not to do so? Or, asking these same questions in the language of rights, does D's population have a right to expect its leaders to respond in kind, and C's population a complementary right to expect D not to attack? The same basic question can be asked in a variety of ways.

The tilt in answering this question is probably in the other direction when compared with the scenario concerning nations A and B. Even if we assume that the attacks on the civilian population are having some military repercussions, it is likely (if there is no gross refugee problem to deal with) that there will be no overwhelming military reason to react immediately, in the way there was in dealing with nation A's chemical attack on B's military forces. In that scenario, B had to do something to prevent an impending defeat. Now, with D, no such defeat is in the offing if it restricts its poison gas counterstrikes to military targets. In the long run, C's poison gas attacks on D's cities, towns, and villages might cause the war to be lost, but in the meantime D has time to work out other solutions to C's immoral actions. Minimally, what it could do is document the poison gas attacks for whatever reckoning might take place after the war. Also, by not responding immediately, it could be taking steps toward making it absolutely clear who is the violator of the

Geneva Protocol. In connection with these steps, it would also have time to appeal to neutrals to get C to stop what it is doing.

But, to make the case even worse, what if, despite all these pressures, C continues to attack D's civilian population with a variety of poison gases? What then should be done? Would D be justified in retaliating? As with the earlier scenario, responding in kind might not work. C may not care much about its own casualties, feeling that its population is not so likely as D's to "crack." But then it is another strong possibility that if D finally did respond, C would back off. No doubt C would not stop its attacks immediately, because it might be perceived as having suffered a defeat. But C could gradually ease off its attacks, or stop them completely, because it would likely see little advantage in continuing them.

If there is any moral plausibility in a civilian counterstrike in this sort of scenario, it would be subject to a variety of provisos. Quietly, through diplomatic channels, it should be made clear to C that the initial counterstrikes are not all-out attacks. Or, again through quiet diplomacy, it should be made clear that the attacks will last only for a period of time, before which D would hope for some private or public conciliatory sign from C. In the end, D might find itself in a ghastly no-holds-barred war as the result of the policy of responding in kind to poison gas attacks. But if D had taken all the steps outlined above (and perhaps others as well) before responding in kind, it is not obvious D would be acting immorally.

All the scenarios discussed thus far allow for the possibility of counterstrikes falling within the moral realm in those circumstances where the enemy is behaving in a grossly immoral fashion. But is it possible to imagine moral uses of these weapons on a first-strike basis? Consider the following scenario. Nation N is a Nazilike regime with a proven record of practicing genocide on several ethnic and racial groups. Its military forces need only to overcome nation O's forces to gather another two hundred million people into its deadly net. If N is successful, it will likely send at least ten million more people to their deaths. Further, success seems to be around the corner. Using conventional weapons only, N is gradually grinding O into submission. N's only military weakness, which happens to be O's strength, is in chemical weaponry. Should O use these weapons to avoid defeat and the genocide that will surely follow? It is certainly tempting to say yes, and to do so not just on utilitarian grounds. Without laying out in detail how such an argument might develop for each kind of ethical theory, we can articulate a duty-based argument along the following lines. "Although we have duties not to use immoral weapons, we have conflicting duties to all those people who would be killed by the N regime. Using poison gas against N's military forces is wrong, other things being equal. But using poison gas is not so great a wrong as allowing N to practice genocide on such a large scale."

Poison Gas and Deterrence

Thus there are situations, albeit not everyday ones, where the use of poison gas is not obviously immoral. They are so extraordinary that strict rules prohibiting the use of these weapons can still be said to be in place. Strict though the rules are, they are not absolute. Even though there have been technological advances involving the reaching and disabling functions of these weapons, these advances have not been so significant as to require an absolute rule prohibiting their use.

But what about deterrence? Should nations be allowed, or even encouraged, to stockpile poison gases to deter their opponents from using these weapons? Certainly many proponents of the big argument would answer this question negatively. Their arguments would follow what are by now familiar lines. Among other things, they would say that when nations have these weapons they will use them, sooner or later. They will also say that since these weapons are mounted on quick-strike and long-range delivery systems, escalation will be easy to start and hard to stop.

Compared to arguments involving nuclear weapons, however, these and related arguments do not ring true. With nuclear weapons the special fear is that deterrence requires a variety of weapons to be put on a trigger-sensitive alert because, if they are not used, they might be lost. The anxiety of holding nuclear weapons is especially high because they can be quickly attacked and destroyed by other nuclear weapons. Of course, it is true that nuclear and poison gas warheads sent on their way by missiles go equally fast. But the special anxiety that attaches to nuclear weapons is not found with their poison gas counterparts. Poison gas weapons attack *people* primarily, not other weapons. If it wants to, a victim nation can afford to wait before it retaliates without the fear that the wait itself will cost it the ability to retaliate. It can afford to wait in a variety of situations. And the cliché "If you have a weapon, you will use it" seems far from the truth. Historical records of poison-gas use suggest a different cliché: "If you don't have it, watch out!"

So, if anything, poison gases seem to be safer deterrent weapons than nuclear weapons. They have become even safer for their users since the development of binary-chemical weapons. These weapons consist of two relatively harmless chemicals that become toxic only when mixed together just before the warheads reach their targets (Barnaby 1984d, 108–9). Also, unlike nuclear weapons, poison gases seem to have a proven record as deterrents. Since World War I they have been used in a variety of wars but primarily, it seems, when one military force has been incapable of responding in kind.

Although poison gases, compared to nuclear weapons, are fairly safe deterrents, they are not completely harmless. There are dangers that need to be noted. One such danger has to do with overstockpiling. Deterrence does not require a nation to outproduce its potential enemies by ratios of three and four to one. Such overproduction suggests aggressive rather than defensive intentions. What adds to the danger are the difficulties involved in monitoring a potential enemy's level of poison gas production. Further, monitoring will become increasingly difficult when the new generation of binary weapons comes on line. Because before they are combined to make lethal mixtures the gases are relatively innocuous, they can be innocently passed off as agricultural chemicals or something of the sort (Boyle 1988, 1087–89). Fear, real or not, about the levels of production can easily lead to escalation (Lundin, Perry Robinson, and Trapp 1988, 101–4). Although the big argument may not be strong enough to carry the day for outright prohibition of poison gases, it is strong enough to point to dangers. This argument suggests that agreements between two nervous nations should include some form of mutual inspection to keep the stockpiles of these weapons low and relatively equal (Goldblat 1988, 347–58).

Another danger pertains to a combination of new technologies. Placing modern poison gases in cluster bombs, as is being done now, makes for an extremely powerful weapon system. Cluster-bomb cannisters afford attackers great flexibility (*Jane's Defence Weekly*, April 30, 1988, 852–53). Such cannisters can reach the enemy via artillery, missiles, aircraft, or helicopters. They can also be programmed to create a variable mix of incendiary, antipersonnel, smoke, and other small bombs (bomblets). Being interchangeable with other bomblets, poison gas bomblets would not create a need for special equipment before they could be used, nor would they create any special transportation problems. Supposedly created as deterrent weapons, poison gas bombs might be used in these other ways once a war starts.

Biological Weapons

The threat biological weapons pose to nations is in one sense greater than and in another sense less than that posed by chemical weapons

(Geissler 1986). It is greater because, in theory, once biological weapons are released, they could spread uncontrollable but not necessarily fatal harm among enemy populations (Thomas and Thomas 1970, 33). But, paradoxically, biological weapons pose less of a threat just because they are uncontrollable. A disease spread among enemy populations could spread to one's own. These weapons have another well-known disadvantage to the user. Unlike chemical weapons, biological weapons are slow acting (Thomas and Thomas 1970, 33). The damage they do may take months or years to take effect. As strategic weapons, they are certainly not so effective as other such weapons found in the arsenals of the major powers. Further, it is too easy to imagine how these weapons could be turned against their user. Any technologically advanced nation employing such weapons against another nation with comparable technologies would have, it seems, little to gain.

The more likely danger is where there is technological asymmetry between two nations. Again, guerrilla warfare comes to mind. Guerrillas could only reply to biological warfare by waging some other kind of dirty war. Further, if biological, as well as chemical, weapons were used against guerrillas, their use would likely be difficult to verify by outside sources. The guerrillas themselves might not even know they are being attacked in this way.

There is a new danger with biological weapons. They can be used to attack not only humans and other animal life but also certain high-technology systems. Evidently these weapons "can cause rapid corrosion or collapse of vital electronic systems" (*Jane's Defence Weekly*, April 30, 1988, 852). What makes them especially dangerous is that their use in this capacity may make it easier to think about using them against living creatures.

Biological Weapons—Use and Deterrence

Scenarios with biological weapons are as easy to imagine as are those with chemical weapons. Thus it is possible to think of circumstances where it would be moral to use these weapons. If responses in kind were the only way to stop an enemy from using biological weapons against military targets, that might be a good reason for doing so. Also, if the initial enemy attacks were aimed more at the civilian population, it might be proper, as a last resort, to respond in kind. To be sure, just because the enemy is using biological weapons is not a sufficient reason for countenancing a retaliatory attack. If the enemy is going to be defeated shortly by other means, these weapons ought to be avoided if for no other reason than their crudity as area weapons. Even if the war is not going to end shortly, but the biological nature of the enemy attack is not decisive, it still might not be proper to respond in kind. Yet, the point is, if the circumstances are right, a nation could find itself using these weapons and doing so on moral grounds.

The deterrent reasons for deploying biological weapons are roughly the same as those for chemical weapons. In contrast to nuclear weapons, both are weapon-deterrent rather than war-deterrent weapons. War-deterrent weapons are so ferocious that having them supposedly deters war itself and also the use of these weapons. But as horrible as chemical and biological weapons are (at least in their present form), they are not so horrible as to deter war. Rather, as deterrents, their primary function is to deter their own use. By having biological weapons in stock, a potential victim nation supposedly deters the aggressor from using them once the war starts.

If a nation were reluctant to deploy such weapons, it could respond not in kind, but in parallel. It could counter against attacks by using biological weapons with, say, chemical weapons. These strategies might work if the attacker had no chemical weapons and the victim nation no biological weapons. The attacks and counterattacks would be, in a sense, parallel to one another. However, if the aggressor nation possessed chemical weapons and had, up to that point not used them, then the parallel response to its attack would probably be seen as an example of escalation. The chances of avoiding this result, and of encouraging the aggressor nation to see the counterattack as an attempt to stop the use of biological weapons, would more likely be enhanced if the response were in kind rather than in parallel. Similarly, deterrence is more likely to work if potential biological-weapons attacks are matched by potential biological-weapons counterattacks.

Talk about using chemical and biological weapons during war and as deterrents has an awful ring to it. No doubt, many chemists would have a guilty conscience if they were put to work creating such weapons, as would many biological and medical professionals if they were similarly put to work on biological weapons. But, if the arguments of this chapter make any sense, it is not obvious why these guilt feelings would be appropriate. If it is necessary to threaten to use, and in some situations to actually use, biological weapons against those who would fight immoral wars, some good people will be needed to design and manufacture them.

CHAPTER EIGHT

Institutional Issues and the Big Argument

Scope of the Military-Industrial Complex

The big argument reminds us that the concept of a military-industrial complex is not imaginary. These complexes are found not only in the United States and the Soviet Union but also in the second-echelon nations. As we have seen, a military-industrial complex almost has to exist within these nations, given the political tensions and the accelerating technological developments of the past half century. But recently these complexes have begun proliferating.

This is not to say that the complexes found in the United States and the Soviet Union are no longer dominant. As new weapons such as advanced fighter planes become increasingly expensive, fewer nations find it possible to produce them. Witness the difficulties Israel had with its Lavi fighter plane (King 1988, 17–18). Even having received U.S. subsidies and having built two prototypes, Israel decided it could not afford to go into production. The plane was simply too expensive. Sweden is having cost problems (as well as accidents) with its Gripen advanced fighter plane (*Jane's Defence Weekly*, December 17, 1988, 1535; Rapp 1989, 203). France too is having a problem with its advanced fighter plane, the Rafale (Fouquet and Isnard 1988, 1103). Because of costs, France has found it difficult to finance the research and production of this plane on its own. One proposed solution is to share these costs with other nations. But eligible partners are being wooed by other nations with their own advanced fighter-plane proposals. So France has not had an easy time of it. There are, then, these pressures to narrow the base of the world's military-industrial complexes and thereby keep both the United States and Soviet Union dominant when it comes to expensive military equipment.

Still, most of the pressures are in the other direction. Whereas after World War II only a handful of nations were in position to produce major military weapons, now the figure is well over 50 (*SIPRI Yearbook* 1988, 206–47; Barnaby 1984e, 154; Starr 1990, 265–67). If weapons of all types are included, then well over 125 nations are producers now. Many of the smaller nations are in the weapons-production business under license from the major producers (the United States, Soviet Union, France, West Germany, and Great Britain) or are upgrading old weapon systems (Campbell 1987, 104; Karp 1988, 196). But increasingly these nations are designing and producing weapons of their own. Iraq, for example, under the pressure of its war with Iran, is presently the biggest chemical-weapons producer in the Middle East (*Jane's Defence Weekly*, February 27, 1987, 336). Operating under these same pressures, Iran has moved from producing small arms, artillery, and airplane spares to producing mini-submarines, missiles, rockets, and even remotely piloted vehicles (Deen, November 28, 1987, 1276–77). Taiwan has recently announced that it has developed and is about to produce a new fighter plane (*Jane's Defence Weekly*, January 7, 1989, 4). Even Malaysia has expressed the desire to produce some of its own defense equipment (*Jane's Defence Weekly*, March 2, 1987, 447).

But producing military equipment also leads to weapon sales to other countries. Witness that Iran, during its war with Iraq, probably bought military equipment from as many as 40 nations (Deen 1988, 1276). Some of these purchases were not directly from producers of military equipment. Very likely much of the equipment Iran purchased from North Korea, for example, came originally from China. But other producing nations also contributed to keeping the Iranian war machine going as long as it did. These include Argentina, Austria, Brazil, Israel, Sweden, Switzerland, Taiwan, and West Germany—as well as the United States in the famous Iran-contra affair. For its part, Iraq received arms from Belgium, China, Egypt, France, Great Britain, Italy, and the United States, with France being the biggest seller (Kemp 1988, 164).

A sense of the number of nations that sell military equipment can be gained by noting that in 1987 Ecuador purchased such equipment from Austria, Canada, Israel, Italy, Great Britain, and the United States; Egypt made purchases from France, West Germany, Italy, the Netherlands, Spain, and the United States; while Nigeria made purchases from Czechoslovakia, France, Italy, Great Britain, the United States, and the

Soviet Union (*SIPRI Yearbook* 1988, 206–55). Finally, India, which is also a producer, receives military equipment from Canada, France, West Germany, Great Britain, the United States, and most of all from the Soviet Union.

Obviously there is big money to be made here; otherwise, all these countries would not be so interested in getting in on the action (Karp 1988; 176–77). In fact, the money involved is so great that allied nations (at least in the West) often find themselves in fierce competition for sales. In 1988, for instance, Great Britain succeeded in making an arms deal with Saudi Arabia worth more than $30 billion over ten years. Its main competitor was the United States. In part, Great Britain won because the U.S. Congress was unwilling (largely because of the Israeli lobby) to sell the Saudis such equipment as F-15 fighter planes and Maverick and Stinger missiles (Deen 1988, 122). In a similar vein, the United States, Great Britain, France, and Italy are constantly competing to sell military equipment, especially to Middle Eastern nations, but to other nations as well (Bruce 1987, 936; *Jane's Defence Weekly*, June 18, 1988, 1195). The competition is not restricted to Western nations. The Soviet Union and many of its satellites compete quite successfully in selling military equipment to Third World countries (Bruce 1987, 936).

The net result of this competition, and the general desire most nations have to be strong militarily, is that international sales of military equipment in 1987 exceeded $35 billion by one estimate, and $50 billion by another (Karp 1988, 177; Sundaram 1988, 1049). Total annual purchases of military equipment—that is, what was bought on the international market and produced indigenously—exceeded $3 trillion (Sundaram 1988, 1049). This last figure represents approximately 5.5 percent of all goods and services produced worldwide (Dunnigan 1983, 348; Sivard 1988, 42; Sivard 1989, 46).

The Impact of the Military-Industrial Complexes

Given this account of the size and extent of the world's military-industrial complexes, the claims of those who defend the big argument do not appear exaggerated. At least when only a few nations produced major military weapons, any appeal for peace could focus on these leading producers. But now, with scores of nations producing these weapons, choking off an ongoing war in some corner on the world becomes increasingly difficult. As Iran discovered during the Iran-Iraq war, somebody was always willing to sell it almost any military equipment it needed.

Advocates of the big argument seem to have the facts right. But the big argument is more than a collection of facts. Part of this argument makes causal claims about military expenditures being dangerous. It is not just that the military-industrial complexes make lots of money but that they act as forces to destabilize world peace. They do this by encouraging nations to buy their new, and not so new, equipment. Also, at times, they sell this equipment clandestinely to groups fomenting war (Karp 1988, 190–91). Further, they apply political pressure to keep the complexes going and to make foreign policy hawkish.

There is another element to the argument as it was described in chapter 1. Each military-industrial complex makes money for the home nation because it employs scientists, engineers, and other professionals and nonprofessionals. In this way it helps keep the local economy going. Further, it has been estimated that research and development generated by the military-industrial complex helps yield exports at a rate about two or three times the amount invested. However—and here is the catch—if the research and development had been in civilian goods, the rate of return might have been as high as ten or fifteen to one (King 1988, 17–18). Not only is the rate of return bad with respect to exports, but what is built by the military-industrial complex helps only remotely to maintain the people's standard of living. There is always some spin-off, so money spent on military equipment may indirectly help people live better lives (Pollack 1989, 1, 8). But their lives, so the argument goes, would be better served if those scientists, engineers, and other professionals were employed directly in the task of how to live in peace rather than how to fight a war (Dumas 1984, 142). In short, funneling the nation's resources through the military-industrial complex is a waste.

Let us look at these various causal claims. The claim that the military-industrial complexes produce a low level of return may well be true. Not even advocates of heavy military spending need deny this. In an ideal world, almost everyone would agree that it would be better if nations did not have to "waste" scientific and engineering talent to design some new bomber or nuclear weapon. Such skills directly applied to solving medical, environmental, educational, housing, and transportation problems would likely do more to help people live better lives (Sivard 1989, 7–13). In the same vein, it would also be preferable if nations did not spend so much money fighting crime. The money spent hiring, training, paying, and equipping police could also be better spent in other ways. It is not as if nations could not think of better ways to spend their money than on defense and crime, if they had a choice in the matter.

However, at least some military spending on their part is seen as a necessity, and not just a waste. If there is waste, it is in the excesses we associate with military spending. If a nation spent more than it needed for defense against potential enemies, then the argument that it is making a poor investment would have some bite to it. But if it spent its money to gain some security against a potential aggressor that would destroy its whole economy (and social fabric), it is somewhat idle to argue that the money spent designing a new artillery piece would get a better return if it were instead spent on designing Chevrolets. No doubt, it is worthwhile for someone to point to heavy opportunity costs when nations spend on behalf of the military. In this regard the big argument serves everyone well. But this, again, need only remind those in charge of spending that they need not stop spending any money on the military, but that they should do so more wisely.

According to the big argument, military-industrial complexes also engage in activities that bring war rather than peace. For one thing, they actively pursue nations to sell them militay equipment and supplies. A related claim is they do so because of the profit motive.

I have already indicated that the facts behind the causal claims are true. Advertising (in magazines such as *Army, Airforce Magazine, Aviation Week and Space Technology, Jane's Defence Weekly,* and *International Defense Review*) is only one of many indications of the intense effort by corporations to sell whatever military establishments might need. Further, no informed person would deny that these corporations have the desire to make money—and lots of it. However, what is disputable is whether these efforts are more likely to cause war than to deter it, and whether this tendency, if present, is a strong one.

If for no other reason, the claim that military-industrial complexes always (mostly? often?) cause war can be seen to be somewhat exaggerated by observing how, as powerful as they are, they wax and wane in accord with other pressures. It is not as if, for example, the U.S. military-industrial complex was powerful enough to be the sole or main author of the heavy military spending during the early years of the Reagan administration. Or, beyond those early years, it is not as if the military-industrial complex was powerful enough to sustain the heavy spending (Stubbing 1987, 46, 52). Rather, after a few years of expansion, nonmilitary political pressures eventually slowed this spending down—and now in the 1990s seem to be sending it into reverse (Jackson 1989, 1153). The rapid growth of the U.S. military-industrial complex itself led, in part, to its downfall. The heady days of the early 1980s led to charges of corruption and waste. Thus, any portrait of the U.S. military-industrial complex as an all-powerful, manipulative monster leading the United

States inexorably to the precipice of war simply cannot account for the facts. The institution itself gets manipulated by the nation's political and economic processes.

What can be said about the U.S. military-industrial complex can equally be said of the military-industrial complexes of other Western countries: military expenditures are such that heavy constraints on military-industrial complexes are obvious (King 1988, 17). If anything, it is the Eastern countries where the military-industrial complexes have historically exhibited a steady growth that suggests they are, or have been until recently, relatively immune to economic and political pressures from other segments of the society (Dumas 1984, 144–45).

Still, although military-industrial complexes are not master institutions literally manipulating the rest of society, they can be dangerous to peace. All one needs to convince oneself of this truth is focus attention on nations (several South American ones will do) where the military has historically controlled the political institutions, and where internal oppression and external wars (for example, the Falkland War of 1982) result. But if the claim of the big argument comes down to merely saying that military-industrial complexes pose serious dangers to the societies where they reside, then the argument's claim comes close to being a truism. Of course, any cluster of institutions coming together to form anything as powerful as a military-industrial complex can endanger a society. It can do so directly by overthrowing the civilian government or more insidiously by undermining it.

Actually, the big argument's claim is concerned with more than pointing to serious dangers and so goes beyond being just a truism. The claim is that today's military-industrial complexes are more dangerous than the comparable institutions existing several decades ago. As we have seen, in contrast to the past, when armies and industry geared up periodically to fight a war, technology has combined with international instability to force nations to develop these permanent military-industrial complexes.

But need anyone who opposes the big argument argue against the claim that these modern complexes are more dangerous than the institutions they replaced? More than likely they are more dangerous, and for just the reasons stated in the big argument. However, it does not follow that military-industrial complexes should be abolished or diminished to the point where they no longer pose this greater danger. These complexes might be more dangerous to nations, but so might many of the political and military situations nations face. It may be, therefore, that the greater danger posed by modern military-industrial complexes is simply something we all have to live with. Unqualified (that is, absolute) pacifists would deny this and would say that no overall good comes from these complexes. Their view is that these institutions simply promote war and do nothing or very little to deter it.

However, these claims are difficult to sustain. It is difficult to look back at history and then argue that war was never or only rarely averted because the potential victim nation was well prepared militarily. Why, one might ask, have the Arab nations attacked Israel so rarely? And why did Stalin not attack Western Europe after World War II? Think also of the use of military force in 1962 when the United States quarantined Cuba (Deitchman 1983, 146).

On the flip side it is not difficult to find examples in history where nations were attacked in large part because they were militarily naked. Think here of the many nations Hitler victimized. Or, more recently, think of one of Iraq's reasons for attacking Iran: namely, that the latter was (supposedly) vulnerable. In other words, although military-industrial complexes are dangerous to their owners, they also apparently serve their owners well on occasion. It is as if nations can live neither with them nor without them.

Tentative Conclusions

The big argument is half right then. Nations, it claims, cannot live with military-industrial complexes. It is half wrong, however, when it concludes that they must live without them. What I am suggesting is that because nations cannot live without them, they had better do what they can to at least mitigate their evil effects. What follows, then, are some recommendations concerned with mitigation.

The first and most obvious is that each nation's military-industrial complex needs to be monitored by other institutions. In Western nations, governmental agencies, dissidents within the complexes, political parties, the mass media, churches, universities, and private organizations can all help do this job (Smith 1988, 160–215). Of course, the reason they all are needed pertains to how military-industrial complexes work. Politicians are often themselves at least part-time members of their military-industrial complex. If jobs are at stake in their section of the country, their role as monitor of the complex is subject to a conflict of interest. In his book *The Power Game*, Hedrick Smith gives some examples.

> Political doves join the scramble, too. Senator Alan Cranston, a big advocate of arms control and the nuclear freeze, supports the B-1

bomber whose prime contract is based in California. Senator Carl Levin
of Michigan, another Pentagon critic, has added money to Army
requests for the M-1 tank which is manufactured in Michigan. Senator
Edward Kennedy and House Speaker Tip O'Neill have backed the F-18
fighter and other projects because Massachusetts gets large subcon-
tracts. Mervyn Dymally, a liberal Democratic member of the Black
Caucus, normally given to low-cost housing and programs for the
poor, has voted for the MX missile because defense plants around his
Los Angeles district mean jobs to his constituents. (177)

No institution or group is totally immune from some sort of significant
conflict of interest. For example, are the media in a community where
tanks are made, and thus where many jobs are at stake, likely to talk at
length about military waste and corruption in their local plant? And is
the university that receives research grants from the military going to
raise too many ethical questions about the military?

In addition to monitoring the military-industrial complexes, some
of the more official institutions can play a regulative role. And here, too,
help needs to come from any and all sources, given the power of the
military-industrial complexes. However, "regulative" is too weak a term
to suggest what is needed. As powerful as these complexes are, control
rather than regulation seems to be what is required. Actually, control
needs to be divided sharply into two parts. The first concerns controlling
the military's influence on foreign affairs, where the military or the
industrial sectors of the complex might, intentionally or not, illegiti-
mately precipitate war. The second concerns procurement and use of
military equipment. It is the first concern to which the big argument
speaks most directly, although supporters of this argument are usually
all too happy to point to corruption and waste in military procurement.
Concerning procurement practices, reform of the U.S. military-industrial complex certainly seems in order. Not only is procurement duplication common, but there have been and still are complaints of excessive
profits being made by corporations belonging to the military-industrial
complex (Smith 1988, 200, 213). There are also complaints about the
low-quality products that complex produces and about the officers who
move too quickly from the military to the business and industrial side
upon retirement. It was, no doubt, too much to expect the U.S. military-
industrial complex to operate efficiently during the heady years of the
early 1980s. But with the future promising only scarcity, perhaps the
military-industrial complex will both reform itself and be reformed by
outsiders, at least to some extent. No doubt reforms of other military-
industrial complexes, such as the corpulent one found in the USSR, are

also in order. Reducing this complex's share of the GNP to something less than 10 percent might help the USSR better serve its people.

So the first suggestion for mitigating the dangers inherent in having a military-industrial complex in one's midst is that various institutions within the society should be encouraged to monitor, regulate, and control it. A second suggestion follows from the first. In some cases, the monitoring, if not the regulation and control, needs to transcend national borders. In 1988–89, for example, West German chemical companies were accused by U.S. intelligence of helping Libya develop the technology to produce poison gases. Such accusations are not always to be believed. They might be part of a campaign to help bring down a foreign leader or to sell more gas masks throughout the world (Lundin, Perry Robinson, and Trapp 1988, 101–4). In this case, however, the accusations were apparently well founded (Doerner 1989, 30–31; German Information Service, January 13, 1989, 1; January 20, 1989, 1–3). But whether they are or not, this example makes clear how an ally, the United States in this case, can play a role in helping another nation control its "rogue" businesses regardless of whether those companies are full-time members or are merely on the fringe of that nation's military-industrial complex. A certain amount of help can also come from independent organizations such as Amnesty International and the Stockholm International Peace Research Institute (SIPRI).

A third suggestion for controlling the arms industry involves cooperation of a different sort. It has been observed on several occasions in this study how the costs of military equipment have risen as technology has moved forward at an accelerating pace. Even when accounting for inflation, the cost of many weapons has risen many times over in the past three decades. Given these trends, it makes sense for allies (Eastern, Western, or whatever) to engage in cooperative ventures on a wide variety of weapons and weapon components (Houwelingen 1988, 273). To be sure, nations have special requirements for certain kinds of weapons, so cooperation is not always possible. But where their requirements are similar, cooperation has the advantage of avoiding costly duplication and providing the participating nations with weapons they all can use. Thus, with such cooperation, there are gains in both cost and efficiency.

The promise of such gains is what is behind the so-called Nunn Amendment (an amendment to the U.S. National Defense Authorization Act of 1986, sponsored by Senators Sam Nunn, William Roth, and John Warner). Under the auspices of this amendment, several NATO countries are cooperating (although several nations have recently pulled out) to develop a frigate for the 1990s (Cevasco 1987, 655; Wood 1987,

644; Starr 1989, 1146–47). Most of these same countries are also working together to develop a 155mm autonomous precision-guided munition (smart artillery shells with the capability of finding and hitting different targets). An identification friend or foe (IFF) system is another project obviously crying for some sort of cooperative effort. This project has also been put under the Nunn Amendment umbrella. A variety of other projects are in the works (Famiglietti 1989a, 346; Starr 1989, 1147–48). The emphasis in all these projects is on starting the cooperation at the earliest stages of development because hardly any country would want to share the progress it has made on a project after spending a king's ransom getting a jump on the competition. So, in being realistic in this regard, the Nunn Amendment seems to be on the right track.

In truth, these suggestions, and any others that might be forthcoming to reform the world's military-industrial complexes, do not satisfy much. If these institutions suffer from diseases, the medicines prescribed here offer little more than symptomatic relief. But, then, this is what it means to only mitigate the problems created by military-industrial complexes. No cures were promised. My argument against the big argument has not been that it is totally wrong. The dangers from military-industrial complexes are serious, as the big argument claims. We ought not to be naive about that. My concern with the big argument is not with its diagnosis, but with its proposed cure. It prescribes radical surgery or even a "final solution" to deal with the problem. From the point of view of those defending the big argument, there would be no regrets if the patient died, only celebration. In contrast, my prescriptions presupppose that there are good reasons for keeping the patient alive and well. Military-industrial complexes serve important societal needs even though the dangers they pose to the societies they serve are greater today than yesterday. Part of my argument in support of this view is that although the dangers from these institutions are great, so are the dangers they deal with. The other part of my argument is that the dangers posed by the military-industrial complexes, serious as they are, are not so great as the big argument suggests.

CHAPTER NINE

Looking Back

The Realist Position

In chapter 1, I asked how both the pacifist and realist positions have changed because of the continuing technological revolution in warfare. Up to now, the pacifist position, as expressed through the big argument, has received most of the attention. This is a reflection of the power of this argument. But now it is time to investigate the power of the realist argument.

Recall that the purpose of this study has not been to investigate all versions of either the realist or pacifist position. Only those versions affected by changes in military technology are being assessed here. So contract realism is being ignored because it has nothing to do with technology. Its adherents argue that ethics finds no place in war because war represents a cancellation of an explicit or implicit contract of cooperation between two or more nations (or groups of people). Similarly, defenders of self-interest realism argue that ethics has no place in war because nations never have ethical relationships with one another. Only self-interest guides how they should behave both before and during war. Technological developments are irrelevant to both of these versions of realism.

Such is not the case with inability realism. Supporters of this position argue that war sets emotions in motion in such a way as to make it impossible for people to control their behavior at least insofar as the enemy is concerned. Because, so the argument goes, ethics requires humans to have some control over their behavior, ethics and war must be incompatible with one another. What we cannot humanly do, we cannot be obligated to do.

If this version of the realist position is to have any application to this study, the inability of people to act ethically in a war setting will have to be a matter of degree. That is, the inability realists would have to argue that modern war makes acting ethically even less likely than wars of the past. Grudgingly, they might even admit that some small wars in history could have been fought in accordance with ethical rules. Perhaps in the old days, the pressures of war were not always so great as to make war and ethics totally incompatible. But today, supposedly, things are different.

Why? Interestingly enough, for many of the same reasons found in the pacifist big argument. For one thing, events in modern war will happen so quickly. There will simply be no time for decision making. Further, even if there is more than a little time, the pressures of war will be so great as to make it unrealistic to expect those fighting the war to think about the niceties of the principles of proportionality and discrimination. Further still, given the heavy casualties modern war will visit upon them, soldiers and civilians alike will find it impossible to control their emotions. All they will be able to think about is "kill or be killed." So the niceties of ethics cannot help but go by the boards.

A related consideration also helps to suppress the expression of any ethical behavior. An inability realist involved in a high-technology war might put it this way, "It is hard enough for us to have any sympathy for our enemy, no matter what kind of war we are fighting. Fear, casualties, reports of atrocities, propaganda, and other considerations all seem to be designed to turn the enemy into monsters and fanatics— and eventually into nonhuman objects. At least with old-fashioned wars fought at close quarters, warriors could view and come to sense the enemy's suffering. However, with modern wars, the battle will increasingly be fought at a distance. The killing and suffering caused by missiles, rockets, airplanes, helicopters, long-range artillery, mines, poison gas, and many other modern weapons will rarely be viewed directly. This will make it easier for us (and the other side) to do the dirty work of war. Yet, although our enemy's suffering will be distanced, our own suffering will not be. If anything, it will be magnified, simply because of the increased devastation of modern war. So we will be more enraged than before, in part because the brutality will be more apparent, but we will not see the brutality we cause. Thus, all of us can imagine, as the war progresses and casualties rise, how each side will become increasingly irrational and how, in turn, ethics will become increasingly irrelevant."

So far, the reasons favoring the inability realist position apply only to the war fighting itself. For those holding this position, once the war starts, little if any ethics could in fact be found there. It could be argued, however, that even if ethics did not have a place during war, it could have a place there before it starts. After all, emotions might not yet be completely out of control before the shooting starts.

It is not easy for the inability realist defenders to reply to this restriction on their position. Because their position emphasizes the volatility of human emotions when blood begins to flow, it implies that calmer times must exist when our emotions are under control. This suggests that inability realism needs to be supplemented by some other version of the realist position—one that would show that ethics has no application at the onset as well as during the process of war. Or the inability realists would have to overcome the inherent difficulties of their position by arguing that emotions, or whatever, make it impossible for nations to consider thinking ethically about war even before it begins.

Here is what that argument might look like as expressed by an imaginary inability realist, who at the same time is in charge of defending his nation against a strong potential enemy. "It takes no great intelligence to see what a modern all-out war might look like. It clearly would be sudden hell in ways that will make past wars seem like skirmishes. My very nation, its culture, its people could all be destroyed quickly and completely. Given what is at stake, I can only pretend to think rationally about ethics, with respect not only to the war itself but also to the preparation for and the start of war. It is true that before war starts we are not taken in by our emotions in quite the way we are during war. Once the war starts, our emotions literally sweep us away and make almost any rational thinking about what is ethical impossible. In the heat of battle men act like beasts. During war, soldiers are innocent of the charges of committing murder, much as is the jealous husband who kills his wife's lover. Both are innocent 'by reason of insanity.' The 'insanity' of peacetime that keeps me from thinking ethically about my nation's defense is, perhaps, more subtle; nonetheless, it is real. When I think about my people and my culture, and how the enemy threatens them, I find myself able, indeed compelled, to do anything—and I mean anything—to rid them of that threat."

By its nature, our inability realist's argument is largely autobiographical. We are being told that his compulsions keep ethics out of the picture. But to be effective, his argument needs to be expressed as something more than a report about his own idiosyncratic compulsions.

If that were all the report were, it would make sense to hospitalize him "by reason of (his) insanity." Thus, in arguing as he does, our inability realist is probably up to something more than merely baring his soul. In his own way he must be speaking for all of us. By implication, his claim must be that none (or at best very few) of us can think and act rationally about matters related to war because the issues surrounding this activity are too close to our heart.

Putting it this way shows how strong his claims are and, correspondingly, how difficult they are to prove. What these claims plausibly suggest is that the pressures of any war make thinking about ethics and acting ethically very difficult. They also suggest that the fear of modern war makes this thinking and acting even more difficult. To that extent, the inability realist position is stronger than it was at an earlier, less technologically dominated, time. However, granting the realist position this point is not enough to save it because, in spite of the difficulties, it is still possible to imagine ethical thinking and acting taking place even in war—let alone before it starts. In fact, many people say they can think and act ethically when they consider war as an option. The realists can reply only that those who suppose they are engaging in these activities are simply fooling themselves. On this account, these allegedly ethically minded people must be rationalizing, or something of the sort. So now, the issue with respect to the realist position before the war starts comes down to a squabble as to how many people really are thinking and acting ethically when they suppose themselves to be doing so.

Roughly the same thing can be said about the war fighting itself. Modern warfare makes thinking and acting ethically more difficult in certain respects. But granting the inability realists this much is not what they need to sustain their position. For them to be correct, nobody (or only very few people) should be able to think and act along these lines. Emotions during war are supposed to be so strong as to completely remove ethics from the battle scene. But what are we to do with those who claim they can think and act ethically during battle? Are they also fooling themselves? Also, in the face of the ethical reasons some military personnel give for why they take prisoners and refrain from randomly shooting civilians, how can the realists know these people are fooling themselves? Obviously they cannot. The opposition has the upper hand in the argument here. People seemingly do engage in ethical thinking about preparing for war, starting wars, and fighting them. And they act on their thinking. Further, their thinking and acting are very similar to the ways they think and act in ethical settings on the home front. Are the realists at this point going to claim that when people engage in ethical thinking about family, friends, school, church, business, etc., they are, once again, fooling themselves?

This overall point can be put somewhat differently. Even if acting ethically in and around modern war settings is clearly more difficult than it is on the home front, inability realists are not thereby shown to be right. One can agree with them about these difficulties, but go on to argue that, because of these difficulties, more effort should be made to make certain military personnel meet the ethical standards of their institution. Codes of ethics need to be taught, discussions about ethics carried out, and threats issued to those inclined to violate the military's ethical rules (Fotion and Elfstrom 1986, 66–84). However this effort of educating military personnel is done, there is no reason to believe that it cannot be effective. The task of teaching ethics to the military may be difficult, but the military has the disciplinary organization to make such teaching possible. In summary, inability realists may be right in focusing on the greater abilities needed to act ethically in modern wars, but they are not right in concluding that this focus shows their position to be correct overall.

The Pacifist Position on Fighting a Modern War

From time to time, I have said that the pacifist position mirrors the realist viewpoint. It does so, but only up to a point. Unlike the realists, pacifists need not be committed to saying that ethics and war exclude one another because no one can act ethically under the emotional pressures of war. All the pacifists need to claim is that once war starts these pressures against acting ethically increase, and that once a *modern* war starts, they increase even more. But pacifists are not limited to talking about the role of emotions in their attempts to show how difficult it is to exhibit ethical behavior in modern war. As we have seen, they claim that the instruments of modern war make fighting an ethical war practically impossible. They also claim that the world's military-industrial complexes make war more likely. Finally, they claim that the opportunity costs of preparing and fighting wars are so great as to make wars morally intolerable.

What I have said thus far about these claims has been of a "yes-and-no" character. Mostly the "yes" portion has had to do with the empirical claims of the pacifists, although at times I have found reason to disagree even here. And the "no" portion has mostly had to do with ethical conclusions the pacifists draw from the facts they cite. Given this "yes-and-no" character of many of my responses, it is useful in this last chapter to summarize what I have said and in the process draw some additional conclusions. I will begin by first discussing war fighting in a modern context. Second, I will discuss the military portion of military-industrial complexes; third, I will examine the industrial portion of these complexes. Finally, I will turn briefly to a discussion of war's opportunity costs and the demand modern technology places on us to be constantly prepared for war. This four-step summary reflects the four parts of the big argument.

In contrast to the view held by pacifists and others that a major future war will be utterly destructive, I have raised some doubts about what will happen. There is uncertainty about the length of such a war if, for example, it were fought between Eastern and Western forces in Europe and elsewhere. Some think it would be short and brutal. Among the advocates of a short-war theory, some suppose there would be escalation to the nuclear level, while others in this group think not. These same short-war theorists also disagree about whether and to what extent chemical and biological weapons would be used. Even the long-term theorists wonder about that. But they speculate as well whether the technologies available to both sides will cancel each other out, rather than have a magnifying advantage for one or the other side. Although there is uncertainty here as well, long-term theorists presumably argue that modern wars will exhibit both destructive and restraint cancellation. Destructive cancellation will occur when both sides employ their high technology in ways to destroy and exhaust each other. Restraint cancellation will occur when each side realizes the cost of committing expensive equipment (for example, $2 billion aircraft carriers, $500 million B-2 bombers, and thousands of $1.5 million tanks). With restraint cancellation, both sides will husband rather than use their most cherished assets.

The long-war theorists point to another consideration in support of their theory. Modern high-technology equipment not only is very expensive but takes a long time to produce. If a war starts between East and West, it is likely, as the short-war theorists also suppose, to be very frenetic initially. In the resulting confusion, both sides are likely to "shoot their wad." Having run out of high- and not-so-high tech ammunition, not to mention fuel and other supplies, they may find themselves bogged down in an old-fashioned war of attrition along an old-fashioned front line.

Thus there is the worst-case scenario of the short-war theorists—that a nuclear war will destroy everything in its wake in a few minutes and the best-case scenario (if that is the right expression) of the long-war theorists that a modern war will not be so different from World War

II and the recent Iran-Iraq war. On one side, then, a portrait is drawn of a totally immoral war no one can win, or, as it might be better put, one that everyone will lose. On the other side, the portrait drawn is of another costly war, but one to which it still makes sense to apply the concepts of just-war theory.

If I am right about all this uncertainty, the pacifist position cannot help but be somewhat undermined—because, after all, it is committed to a form of worse-case thinking. In summary form, the argument says that if the major military powers pursue arms escalation policies, a war will inevitably break out; and when it does, it will inevitably lead to total destruction. Right now, of course, I am focusing only on the destruction portion of this argument in denying inevitability. And about that portion, no one need deny that the worst-case scenario could become a reality. Indeed, this may be all the pacifists need insist on to sustain their position. But if their rhetoric carries them beyond this to talking about how modern war will inevitably be totally destructive, they may be wrong for several reasons. In addition to the reasons mentioned—of technologies cancelling each other out, of high costs, and of slow production lines—one needs also to be reminded of the so-called positive technologies. In some ways, these technologies in the form of smart bombs and missiles may make it easier for the military to fight its wars ethically.

Another consideration weakens the big argument. It has to do with the "don't-you-realize" element implicit in the argument. Sometimes this element becomes explicit. "Don't you realize what would happen once nuclear weapons started to fall on the Central Front?" "Don't you realize how many civilians would be killed once a conventional war between the Soviet Union and the United States got under way?" and "Don't you realize what would happen to the environment once . . .?" It is as if, in expressing their views, the advocates of the big argument believe that most of us have not thought about these issues at all or have been watching too many John Wayne movies. In either case, we (that is, those who disagree with them) evidently lack an appreciation of what wars are like—how utterly horrible they are. Once we come to an appreciation of what is really involved in fighting a modern war, presumably we will be so overwhelmed as to abjure war. The increase in the horror of war, or at least our appreciation of its horror, is supposed to increase our abhorrence of war proportionally.

Let the point be granted that modern wars are more horrible than their predecessors. What follows? If other things were equal, the pacifists' claim that we should abjure war would make more sense. Why engage in an activity whose costs in life and material are much greater than in the past?

But everything is not equal. Not only can modern wars kill more people but they have the potential to deprive people more quickly of the things they have historically gone to war to protect. As I have argued, both the costs of fighting and not fighting a war may be higher today than yesterday.

No doubt military powers are finding it difficult to subjugate people in some cases (for example, witness both the first and the second Vietnam wars and the Afghanistan war). It is also true that others are finding it difficult to keep those who have been subjugated in that state permanently (as the Israelis are finding out with the Palestinians). Nonetheless, because of their greater reach, mobility, and destructive power, modern military forces have the capability to take over nations and territories faster than before. Although a nation's own military may be more dangerous to its health than before, so may other nation's military forces. The dangers are greater both internally *and* externally. By pointing almost exclusively to the quite real internal dangers, the big argument fails to fully appreciate the external ones.

What, overall, is to be said about the pacifists' big argument with respect to fighting wars? It exaggerates. First it does so with respect to the certainty of modern wars occurring and, perhaps, even exaggerates about the extent of the horrors of these wars. Second, it exaggerates about the overall costs of war by focusing almost exclusively on the costs of the wars themselves, without having much to say about the costs of being conquered quickly and perhaps permanently by a modern military machine.

Exaggeration aside, however, the big argument still retains much of its force. Modern wars may not be so destructive as some forms of the argument suggest, but the argument's warnings are still worth listening to. What with the availability of nuclear weapons, poison gases, biological weapons, and long-reach and fast-strike conventional weapons, any future high-technology war could easily spin out of control. Most just-war theorists would not disagree here. As a result, they would be more reluctant, when compared with the past, to recommend going to war. They would likely also insist on placing more restraints on the military once such a war starts. Overall, the dangers of modern war would make just-war theorists more wary. So there is a kind of convergence between the two positions. However, just-war theorists would still insist that wars can be started for moral reasons and that they can still be fought morally. Morality for just-war theorists can still be found at the doorway of and inside war.

The Military

If the big argument is guilty of exaggeration concerning war itself, is it also guilty of exaggeration in talking about the military establishment? Yes, even here. As Samual Huntington indicated in his classic work *The Soldier and the State*, the military mind is not necessarily and, in fact, not especially, war mongering (1957, 59–79). The military mind urges preparedness for war, but it cautions against starting one. To be sure, how a military feels about starting wars will vary from nation to nation. But it is simply a false picture of the military to characterize it uniformly as a war-mongering institution. If Huntington is to be believed, the military is too sensitive to the pitfalls and uncertainties of battle, more so than politicians, to be always out looking for trouble.

Yet even if the big argument is wrong about how the military mind works, it may not be wrong about the effects the military mind has on precipitating war. What may be important is not so much what the military mind actually intends, but what its policies unconsciously lead to. Military preparedness by one nation supposedly leads to feelings of insecurity by a potential enemy, which in turn leads that nation up the road to preparedness. Once started, the cycle of preparedness and insecurity escalates upward to economic ruin or war. This is the familiar pattern of thinking built into the big argument, with which we have been dealing throughout this study.

Is this pattern of what is likely to happen also an exaggeration? In part, yes. That the preparedness urged traditionally by the military can get out of control suddenly or gradually (as is more likely in modern times) is beyond question. That it therefore bears watching by the other institutions in the society is also beyond dispute. However, to view the process of preparedness as inexorably leading to an unwanted war is overly simplistic because, in certain circumstances, the process can move (and now in the 1990s seems to be moving) in the opposite direction. So the solution to avoiding an unwanted war is not necessarily to abolish or ravage the military. Rather, it is to find the conditions under which preparedness does and does not diminish the chances of such a war occurring, and then act accordingly.

Putting aside the political, economic, and social conditions that might lead to an unwanted war, the weapons identified in earlier chapters as most likely to trigger wars are the strategic ones. Bombers (like the B-1, B-2, and Blackjack), intercontinental and intermediate-range ballistic missiles (launched from the ground, in the air, or from submarines), cruise missiles (launched from the ground, in the air, from submarines or surface craft), attack aircraft carriers, and long-range fighter bombers all fall into this category of strategic weapons, along with some other weapon systems. As became evident in chapters 5 and 6, although these weapons can be built in the name of defense, they are almost indistinguishable from the weapons a nation would want to build if it were planning a war of aggression. This is part of the problem. The other part is that these strategic weapons also seem to have genuine military functions for nations not intent on starting a war. The fear these weapons engender as instruments of retaliation very likely gives potential aggressors pause.

There is a related problem. A nation like the United States makes technological leadership part of its deterrent military policy. Insofar as strategic weapons are concerned, this leadership means it can be viewed as acting like an aggressor because it leads in designing, building, and then deploying state-of-the-art weapons. Starting soon after the Cold War was "declared," the United States led with the development of long-range strategic bombers (B-36, and later the B-47 and B-52) and with the development of long-range, nuclear-armed missiles launched from submerged submarines. Later, in again what could be viewed as following aggressive policies, the United States developed the multiple independently targetable re-entry vehicle (MIRV), which permits one missile to do the job of many by sending several targeted warheads off in different directions. In this sense, MIRVs are true strategic-force multipliers (and moneysavers to boot). The United States also led in developing the cruise missile and now in stealth technology—with not only the B-2 but also the stealth fighter plane (the F-117) and other weapons (Sweetman 1988a, 1266).

In defense of the United States' building all these weapons, it could be argued that it had no choice. Although it demobilized to some extent after World War II, the Soviet Union continued to maintain what seemed to many countries an overly large military machine. Not being able to maintain a quantitatively equivalent machine for both economic and political reasons, the United States and its Western allies took the shortcut of investing in strategic weapons. It appears now, late in this century, that the USSR also could not afford its large military commitment. Nonetheless, the machine was in place, and the United States, in particular, responded the only way it could. It went for quality over quantity in weaponry, even if that meant it might be perceived by a paranoid USSR to be a potential aggressor. That is the American argument.

Of course, from the USSR's point of view it was not paranoia that drove it to chase the United States in raising the levels of its own weapons technology. At the time, the United States' B-36, armed as it was with nuclear weapons, was a formidable weapon; the stealth twins, the F-117 and B-2, are formidable; and the stealth cruise missile promises to be an equally formidable weapon (Sweetman 1988a, 1266; Sweetman 1990, 413).

In the end, the question is not whether the United States was historically justified in maintaining its technological lead in strategic weapons, but whether such a lead can find ethical justification under certain circumstances. I would suggest the following answer. It is not necessarily unethical to engage in such technological one-upmanship. To freeze a nation's technology in place in strategic weapons or to allow this technology to languish for even a few years is tantamount to strategic unilateral disarmament. More than that, if the deterrent power of a nation's strategic weapons relies on quality rather than quantity, it is practicing unilateral disarmament on a quick-time basis if it rests on its laurels. So if, as I have argued earlier, unilateral disarmament is not necessarily a good thing, it would follow that quality may need to be maintained. In turn, this means that new weapons may need to be developed for certain nations to maintain a credible deterrent against a larger foe.

However, because these deterrent weapons are also ideally suited for aggression, certain safeguards in their production and deployment should be kept in mind. They obviously should not be produced in numbers large enough to suggest aggressive intent. Further, older weapons should be phased out as newer ones come on line—again so as not to give the impression that a large number of dangerous weapons are being massed for some evil purpose. As has already been suggested, other steps might be taken, including bilateral agreements to limit the number of strategic weapons, mutual inspection of these weapons, and the like. Indeed, because certain kinds of strategic weapons exist in such large numbers, there is a special urgency to pursue such agreements. In theory, if bilateral agreements could be made to totally eliminate whole classes of strategic weapons, such agreements should be made. In practice, however, because such agreements will not likely become the norm, countries like the United States should not be automatically condemned for designing and deploying the B-2 or some other modern strategic weapon. Condemnation especially should be withheld if the rest of a nation's military establishment is not deployed in an aggressive posture. Thus, if a nation's tactical offensive weapons (for example, tanks, mechanized infantry, bridging equipment) are not deployed in sufficient numbers to threaten a potential enemy with a war of aggression, its overall military posture should not be considered aggressive in nature, even though it is deploying new and powerful strategic weapons.

This discussion should not be taken as an expression of approval of the B-2 bomber or any other particular "fancy" strategic weapon system. It may, in fact, be that most of the missions the B-2 is designed to perform could be equally well performed by some *not very* sophisticated aircraft firing *very* sophisticated standoff missiles (Deitchman 1983, 250). It may also be that the U.S. Air Force is still suffering from a "12 O'clock High" syndrome of wanting its pilots to carry their bombs over their targets the way it was done in the glory days of World War II. Whatever the reason, money and resources might have been saved if the United States had deployed its technological prowess more in the direction of missiles rather than aircraft. Then again, the B-2 might be just the thing to keep the USSR's defenses playing catch-up for the next decade or two (Thurman 1988, 517–18). It is not any one particular strategic weapon system I wish to defend here, but the principle that there is nothing inherently wrong with developing and deploying certain kinds of strategic weapons in certain limited numbers. Because these weapons have an inherent ambiguity as both deterrents and weapons of aggression, the point is a touchy one. It is difficult to make a clear-cut case that it is morally permissible to possess these weapons. But that is just the kind of case I am trying to make. Given the proper hedges, my argument is that in certain circumstances it is not only ethically permissible to possess these weapons, but also ethically permissible to take the lead in developing them.

Industry

Does the big argument exaggerate in its claims about the dangers of the industrial portion of the military-industrial complexes? If one dwells on the almost unbounded magnitude of the profit motive in capitalist countries and on the power or profit motive in Marxist countries, it would seem not. If one couples these "grasping" tendencies with the observations made earlier that the industrial portion of these institutions seems to be proliferating, that they often work in consort with the military to serve the needs of the complex rather than of the country, and that they also work with the politicians to serve the complex rather than the country, then the dangers seem serious. More than that, they seem to be causing danger to society in return for doing no one but themselves any good. It is as if the industrial portion of these complexes represents pure evil.

However, consider the following three points. First, those who produce baby food also want to maximize their profits, as are those who build churches, and those who manufacture medicines. It is not the profits as such that make weapons producers and traders seem evil. They are usually perceived as evil because their profits are placed against a backdrop of the idea that war itself is evil. But, second, if not all wars are evil, then the arms producers can be seen as something other than "merchants of death." One hardly needs to be reminded that just wars cannot be fought with justice alone. Further, if the machines and weapons of war actually deter war in some cases, then what has been produced has led to some good. Third, given modern technology, it would be very dangerous to dismantle the industry that supports the military—even if peace seems to be on the horizon. Once dismantled, the specialist skills needed to invent, design, and produce new weapons would go to other industries. It would be difficult (especially for a nation working within a framework of a free-market rather than a command economy) to put it all back together even if an emergency arose, and even if the emergency lasted over several years. If, in the meantime, other nations' military-industrial complexes have been doing their scientific research and producing weapons of various kinds, the technological gap that inevitably would develop would not likely ever be overcome.

Thus if a nation is seeking such goods as security and freedom, the industrial side of these institutions is necessary. Further, it is necessary that the industrial side be there, on the job, all the time. More than in the past, any closing down of a nation's arms industry would likely be fatal. But having cleansed the arms industry image by saying these things, and thereby having mitigated the bad image given the industry by the big argument, the serious dangers posed by this industry remain. The image cleanup may well defuse the big argument's rhetoric, but not the main punch of the argument itself. After all, it could be argued, even vigilantes sometimes do some good. But that hardly is an argument for supporting them institutionally.

Does, then, the arms industry do more harm than good? Does it do enough harm as against good so as not to deserve support as an institution? Further, do arms dealers add to the harm done?

Just as these institutions and the people who support them sometimes act as deterrents to war by providing weapons to potential victim nations, no doubt they sometimes act to start wars by providing weapons to aggressors. But to see the arms industry as *the* major war-causing engine is simplistic. Wars are caused by religious and ideological differences, nationalistic megalomania, and economic difficulties. Wars are also caused by politicians who wish to distract their people from difficult domestic problems, who miscalculate the costs of war, and who want to gain revenge for their nation about real and imagined past injustices. It is true that the arms industry may feed on and encourage this nationalistic megalomania and may also influence the politicians who look to war as a distraction from domestic problems. In this secondary sense the industry may cause an unwanted war—although, as I have argued, it may also enable a nation to fight a just war or maintain the peace.

Rather than causing unwanted wars, the major faults of the arms industry are probably in the direction of encouraging corruption, dishonesty, and waste. As we have seen, some military equipment is very expensive and very technical. So expensive and so technical, in fact, that perhaps only one company can be found to make an aircraft carrier, an atomic submarine, a stealth bomber, a main battle tank, a space shuttle, an intercontinental missile, or an advanced, medium-range, air-to-air missile. With the lack of competition for producing some of these weapons, it is difficult for the military and the government to impose quality standards on the manufacturer. And with so much money (and jobs) at stake in producing some of these weapon systems, it is tempting for the manufacturers to bribe both the military and the politicians to keep and renew their contracts. It is also easy for them to prevent inspectors from doing an overly thorough job watching over quality control.

Unfortunately, as we have seen, these problems are not likely to go away as the level of technology and cost rises. Apparently they go with the territory. All nations can hope to do is watch over and control their arms producers as best they can. But if these are the main problems posed by these producers, they are not so serious as it seemed at first. Corruption, waste, and dishonesty are management problems. They are not in the same league as having a rogue institution within the society with the power to literally trigger a war. To suppose that the arms industry is such a rogue institution has, I have been arguing, the smell of scapegoating.

Opportunity Costs

Like its claims about the horrible nature of modern war, about the military, and about industry, the big argument's claims about opportunity costs are also exaggerated. But like these other claims, it would be wrong to exaggerate how exaggerated the big argument's claims are.

Yes, there are heavy opportunity costs when nations invest 2 percent, 6 percent, or even more than 10 percent of a nation's GNP on the military (Sivard 1989, 50–52). Yes, money saved on the military could be used to pay off a large national debt, reduce taxes, or better serve the society's other institutions (Beatty 1990, 74–82). And, yes, the return in terms of creating some condition of welfare to society is probably less with military spending than it is for spending on education, housing, medicine, and food. But, no, it is not as if nations build military weapons primarily because watching aircraft carriers glide over the sea and bombers fly low in the sky engenders national pride or gives people aesthetic pleasure. At least in some cases they build and deploy these weapons because they see, or think they see, an obvious need for having them. So if the money spent on the military is spent efficiently and sensibly, which of course it often is not, it is wrong to suggest that the opportunity costs are too high. Indeed, the opportunity costs of not spending money wisely on a military machine might well be the loss of freedom or some other value cherished by a society. Taking everything into account, then, it may be that the opportunity costs of not being prepared for war are even higher than those of being prepared.

Some Closing Thoughts

Although in the end I am giving a positive answer to the question "Is the pacifist position stronger today than it was a generation or two ago?" few things said in this study will make most pacifists and their allies happy. After all, although I have done so reluctantly, I have suggested that in certain circumstances it is morally permissible to keep strategic weapons in one's military arsenal. In certain circumstances, I have argued, it is even morally permissible to invest money toward improving these weapons. As if that were not bad enough, I have gone so far as to praise certain weapons—those possessing more defensive features. Also, although I have criticized the world's military-industrial complexes, my recommendations for reforming them would not excessively distress those who live and thrive inside these institutions.

As if these concessions to war preparedness were not enough, I have also suggested that there may be times, rare though they be, when the actual use of nuclear weapons, poison gas, and other generally admitted immoral weapons is morally permitted. Part of the reason for holding such a position is that there are times when using these weapons does more good than harm. The other part has to do with deterrence. If a nation makes it clear to those other nations who might threaten it that it might use these weapons, the credibility of its deterrent is not likely to be questioned. So my reliance on deterrence theory, or at least a variant of it, is another reason defenders of the big argument might not be happy with the views expressed in this study.

In effect, my position insists on a strong and healthy military establishment when danger is present and even when it is on the horizon. And that too goes against one of the main presuppositions of the big argument. That presupposition sees the military as a monolithic and austere institution. It sees it as "the military." Further, it suggests that the military brings about far more harm than good. It brings about some of these effects consciously because its main concern is to serve itself rather than the nation. But it also brings about harmful effects unconsciously. Neither the military nor the nation as a whole often sees the gradual and far-reaching effects of militarism or, as it might be called, warism (Cady 1988, 4–8). Because of all these bad effects, according to this view, the military has to be rated overall an unworthy institution. It is best eliminated rather than reformed.

In contrast, I would have it reformed because it is worth reforming. It gives the society important services. Further, I have argued that there is no such thing as "the military" any more than there is some one thing called "modern military technology." The military is a complex institution made up of people and organizations with varied views. As to their weapons, some are more dangerous than others insofar as ethics is concerned. However, overall, although this institution and its weapons are dangerous, they can be managed.

In fact, there is recent evidence concerning the military's manageability. Starting in the middle 1980s, military budgets have been shrinking. The realization that the direct and indirect costs of maintaining high-profile military establishments create heavy burdens seems to be a factor in the equation. Also the fact that several wars ended or are winding down is another factor. Not only have the USSR and the United States begun shrinking their military spending, but so have a wide variety of countries, including the Warsaw Pact countries, Canada, France, Israel, and the Netherlands (*Jane's Defence Weekly*, January 21, 1989, 86–88; January 28, 1989, 116–17; February 11, 1989, 206; Allen-Frost 1989, 46; Famiglietti 1989b, 784–85; Hobson 1989, 788; Isnard 1989, 786; Lok 1989, 786). If anything, the events of late 1989 in Eastern Europe have accelerated this trend of shrinking military budgets (*Jane's Defence Weekly*, January 6, 1990, 18–19).

It is open to question how long this downturn in military expenditures will continue. Even if it does for a while, there is the different question as to whether near-future developments in military technology will once again trigger an escalation of fear and military spending (O'Connell 1989, 309). The developments I have in mind in raising this question are both horizontal and vertical. Horizontal developments have to do with the proliferation of technology to smaller nations so that they come to have the weapons the big nations have. Here, among others, we naturally think of nuclear weapons, poison gases, and biological weapons as well as the missiles useful for their delivery (Lennox 1989, 1384–85). Vertical developments include such technologies as strategic defenses against nuclear missile attacks, stealth weaponry, and also new developments in chemical and biological weaponry.

About the horizontal developments, some degree of pessimism is appropriate. It is difficult to imagine how political and economic pressures will stop much of this proliferation in the long run. There are too many divergent sources for too much war-making material for proliferation not to continue. Also skills are proliferating. Nations no longer need depend on other nations to give them their weaponry. As we saw earlier with Iran and Iraq, these countries went into the business of producing military weapons for themselves; and there is no indication, now that their war is over, that they are going out of business soon. So in a few years, as more countries gain access to these weapons, a kind of unfocused instability will exist: with weapons being produced everywhere, many nations will not always be able to figure just where the next threat is coming from. The fear engendered from this situation will tempt countries to take military action against one another before they perceive that the situation gets out of control (Ottaway 1988, 1, 6). The hope here is that the reduction in spending, especially among the major powers, will slow down this proliferation and that, therefore, no short-term instability will occur. But clearly this is only a hope.

As to vertical developments, I have said it is not necessarily unethical to take the lead here. If a nation is overmatched quantitatively by a potential aggressor nation, it has a perfect right to try to balance things by overmatching the potential aggressor qualitatively. In concrete terms, it was not necessarily unethical of the United States to match the Soviet Union's many SS-20s with a fewer number of more capable Pershing II and cruise missiles. This does not mean the United States should have deployed these missiles. There might have been other reasons for keeping them in their boxes someplace in the United States or perhaps for not manufacturing them in the first place. As it turned out, it appears that more good came from deploying them than not. However, even if this were not the case, it follows that if quantity and quality can be put on a theoretical balance sheet, both the quantitatively and the qualitatively superior nations can complain about the other overdoing its advantage. That is, just as the nation ahead in quality can complain when its potential opponent is building too many tanks and has too many artillery pieces, so the opponent can complain when its potential enemy is deploying too many types of fancy high-technology weapons. Thus, if we assume for the moment that neither nervous nation is planning a war of aggression, there are good reasons for both sides to show restraint with regard to their respective deployment practices. Evidently, too much of a good thing, either quantitatively or qualitatively, is just as bad as too little.

About these vertical developments, there is some reason for optimism. Lower military budgets should put ceilings on the number of new weapon systems that can be deployed as well as on the size of military establishments. Openness should also help. Nations often have felt the need to escalate to a higher technological level because worse-case scenario thinking is appropriate in an environment where one side does not know what the other is doing. If, in these and other ways, the major military powers back off step-by-step, my pessimistic assessment of horizontal developments may be off its mark. If the big nations take a few steps backward, the smaller ones may also be less inclined to start fights among themselves—especially if the big nations do not support small-nation aggression. So even though high technology will inevitably proliferate, this trend need not necessarily mean that wars themselves will flourish. That is, there might be more wars in the future because of proliferation, but perhaps not so many as there might otherwise have been had proliferation been encouraged by the major military powers of the world as well.

What these speculations about the near and middle future suggest is that the big argument will need to be assessed once again in a generation or so—or sooner. Given its nature, the big argument is an on-going one. As of now, I have argued that the big argument has more clout today than it had a generation ago. Technology has changed war and changed, as a result, how we ethically assess it. But it has not changed it so much that wars cannot be started and fought in accordance with ethical principles. Insofar as the big argument suggests otherwise, it is wrong. But just as it has more clout today, it may have still more clout a generation from now. Both horizontal and vertical developments may get so out of control that the occasions for entering wars of the future with justice on one's side will be fewer in number than they are even now. But who knows what surprises technology will have for us in the future? It may be that by the next generation, robotic tanks and airplanes will be doing the fighting for us, and in that sense wars may become less inhumane.

References and Bibliography

Abramowitz, Jeff. 1987. "CW Changes the Rules of Middle East War." *Jane's Defence Weekly* (Nov. 7): 1063–69.

Allen-Frost, Peter. 1989. "Compromise Cut in Israeli Defence Budget." *Jane's Defence Weekly* (Jan. 14): 46.

Army, U.S. 1988. *1988–89 Green Book: The Year of Training.* Arlington, Va.: Association of U.S. Army.

Art, Robert J. 1985. "Between Assured Destruction and Nuclear Victory: The Case for the 'Mad Plus' Posture." *Ethics* 95 (April): 497–516.

Barnaby, Frank. 1984a. "New Members of the Nuclear Club." In *Future War: Armed Conflict in the Next Decade,* edited by Frank Barnaby, 44–55. London: Michael Joseph.

———. 1984b. "New War Technologies." In *Future War: Armed Conflict in the Next Decade,* edited by Frank Barnaby, 56–71. London: Michael Joseph.

———. 1984c. "The Battlefield of the Future." In *Future War: Armed Conflict in the Next Decade,* edited by Frank Barnaby, 72–82. London: Michael Joseph.

———. 1984d. "Chemical and Biological Warfare." In *Future War: Armed Conflict in the Next Decade,* edited by Frank Barnaby, 106–13. London: Michael Joseph.

———. 1984e. "The Arms Trade." In *Future War: Armed Conflict in the Next Decade,* edited by Frank Barnaby, 148–58. London: Michael Joseph.

Barnaby, Frank, and E. Boeker. 1982. *Defence Without Offence: Non-Nuclear Defence for Europe.* Peace Studies Paper No. 8. West Yorkshire, Eng.: Bradford University.

Beatty, Jack. 1990. "A Post-Cold War Budget." *Atlantic* (February): 74–82.

Bertram, Cristoph. 1988. "US-Soviet Nuclear Arms Control." In *SIPRI Yearbook 1988: World Armaments and Disarmament*, 301–3. Oxford: Oxford University Press.

Biddle, Wayne. 1987. "Star Wars: the Dream Diminished." *Discover* (July): 26–30, 32–35, 38.

Blake, Nigel, and Kay Pole, eds. 1983. *Dangers of Deterrence: Philosophers on Nuclear Strategy*. London: Routledge and Kegan Paul.

Blake, Nigel, and Kay Pole, eds. 1984. *Objections to Nuclear Defence: Philosophers on Deterrence*. London: Routledge and Kegan Paul.

Boyle, Dan. 1988. "An End to Chemical Weapons: What are the Chances?" *International Defense Review* 21 (September): 1087–89.

Braude, Jonathan. 1988. "CW to be 'Standard Military Practice.' " *Jane's Defence Weekly* (Aug. 27): 357.

Bruce, James. 1987. "Arms Sales Race in the Middle East." *Jane's Defence Weekly* (May 16): 936.

Bruce, James, and Tony Banks. 1988. "Growing Concern over Iraqi Use of CW." *Jane's Defence Weekly* (Sep. 24): 715.

Burke, John T. 1988. "The Firepower Revolution." *Army* (November): 50–60.

Cady, Duane L. 1988. "Unveiling Warism." *Concerned Philosophers for Peace Newsletter* 8 (April): 4–8.

Campbell, Christy. 1987. "Land Warfare: The Arms Industry Spread Worldwide." In *The Orbis Military Yearbook: 1987*, edited by Ashley Brown and Reg Grant, 104–15. London: Oriole Publishing.

Cevasco, Frank. 1987. "The Initiative in Action." *Jane's Defence Weekly* (Apr. 11): 655, 657.

Cohen, Avner, and Steven Lee. 1986. "The Nuclear Predicament." In *Nuclear Weapons and the Future of Humanity: The Fundamental Questions*, edited by Avner Cohen and Steven Lee, 1–37. Totowa, N.J.: Rowman and Allanheld.

Cohen, Sheldon M. 1989. *Arms and Judgment: Law, Morality, and the Conduct of War in the Twentieth Century*. Boulder, Colo.: Westview Press.

Creel, Herrlee G. 1953. *Chinese Thought: From Confucius to Mao Tse-Tung*. Chicago: University of Chicago Press.

Deen, Thalif. 1987. "Iran—Meeting its Arms Requirements." *Jane's Defence Weekly* (Nov. 28): 1276–77.

———. 1988. "Saudi Deal a 'Slap' for Congress." *Jane's Defence Weekly* (July 23): 122.

Defense Monitor. 1988a. "After the INF Treaty: U.S. Nuclear Buildup in Europe." Vol. 17, No. 2.

———. 1988b. "U.S.-Soviet Military Facts." Vol. 17, No. 5.

Deitchman, Seymour J. 1983. *Military Power and the Advance of Technology: General Purpose Military Forces for the 1980s and Beyond*. Boulder, Colo.: Westview Press.

Doerner, William R. 1989. "On Second Thought: A Tale of Intrigue and Deceit Unfolds Over Libya's Chemical-arms Plant." *Time* (Jan. 23): 30–31.

Donaldson, Thomas. 1985. "Nuclear Deterrence and Self-Defense." *Ethics* 95 (April): 537–48.

Dumas, Lloyd. 1984. "The Economics of Warfare." In *Future War: Armed Conflict in the Next Decade,* edited by Frank Barnaby, 125–47. London: Michael Joseph.

Dunnigan, James F. 1983. *How To Make War: A Comprehensive Guide to Modern Warfare.* New York: Quill.

Famiglietti, Len, and Paul Beaver. 1988. " 'Vital' V-22 Rolls Out to Warm USMC Reception." *Jane's Defence Weekly* (June 4): 1095.

Famiglietti, Len. 1989a. "Nunn Success Prompts US Review." *Jane's Defence Weekly* (Mar. 4): 346.

————. 1989b. "V-22 Among Victims as Bush Wields Budget Axe." *Jane's Defence Weekly* (May 6): 784–85.

Fotion, Nicholas, and Gerard Elfstrom. 1986. *Military Ethics: Guidelines for Peace and War.* London: Routledge and Kegan Paul.

Fouquet, David, and Jacques Isnard. 1988. "EFA/Rafale Collaboration Mooted." *Jane's Defence Weekly* (Nov. 5): 1103.

Fung, Yu-Lan. 1952. *A History of Chinese Philosophy.* Princeton, N.J.: Princeton University Press.

Geissler, Ehrhard. 1986. *Biological and Toxin Weapons Today.* New York: SIPRI; Oxford, Eng.: Oxford University Press.

German Information Service. 1989. "Genscher Calls for Total Chemical Weapons Ban," "Authorities Study New Leads in Libyan Affair." *The Week in Germany* (Jan. 11): 1.

————. 1989. "Bonn: Indication of Chemical Weapons Plant," "SPD Charges Bonn with Coverup in Libyan Affair." *The Week in Germany* (Jan. 20): 1–3.

Gervasi, Tom. 1987. *Soviet Military Power: The Pentagon's Propaganda Document, Annotated and Corrected.* New York: Vintage Books, a division of Random House.

Goldblat, Jozef. 1988. "Multilateral Arms Control Efforts." In *SIPRI Yearbook 1988: World Armaments and Disarmaments,* 347–71. Oxford: Oxford University Press.

Goodin, Robert E. 1985. "Nuclear Disarmament as a Moral Certainty." *Ethics* 93 (April): 641–58.

Green, Peter. 1970. *Alexander the Great.* New York: Praeger Publishers.

Han, Woo-keun. 1970. *The History of Korea.* Seoul, Korea: Eul-Yoo Publishing Company.

Hannig, N. 1981. "The Defense of Western Europe with Conventional Weapons." *International Defence Review* (November): 1439–43.

Hardin, Russell, and John J. Mearsheimer. 1985. "Introduction" (to "Symposium on Ethics and Nuclear Deterrence"). *Ethics* 95 (April): 411–23.

Hartle, Anthony E. 1989. *Moral Issues in Military Decision Making*. Lawrence: University Press of Kansas.

Hobbes, Thomas. 1968/1651. *Leviathan*. Edited by C. B. MacPherson. New York: Penguin Books.

Hobson, Sharon. 1989. "Canada Cancels Submarine Plans." *Jane's Defence Weekly* (May 6): 788.

Holmes, Robert L. 1989. *On War and Morality*. Princeton, N.J.: Princeton University Press.

Houwelingen, Jan van. 1988. "Defence Co-operation Is Europe's Future." *Jane's Defence Weekly* (Feb. 13): 273.

Huntington, Samuel. 1957. *The Soldier and the State*. Cambridge, Mass.: Belnap Press of Harvard University Press.

Isnard, Jacques. 1989. "French Budget Splits Government." *Jane's Defence Weekly* (May 6): 786.

Jackson, James H. 1989. "Reshaping of the Defence Industry." *Jane's Defence Weekly* (Nov. 25): 1153–55.

Jane's Defence Weekly. Feb. 27, 1988. "Iraq Now Middle East's Biggest Chemical Weapon Producer," 336.

Jane's Defence Weekly. Mar. 2, 1988. "Malaysia May Produce Own Defence Equipment," 445.

Jane's Defence Weekly. Apr. 30, 1988. "Soviet Intelligence—A New Generation of CB Munitions," 852–53.

Jane's Defence Weekly. June 18, 1988. "Abrams 'Made in UK' Offer to VSEL," 1195.

Jane's Defence Weekly. July 16, 1988. "Surikov: How We'll Counter SDI," 86–87.

Jane's Defence Weekly. Dec. 3, 1988. "B-2: The US Air Force Rolls Out the Future," 1376–77.

Jane's Defence Weekly. Dec. 17, 1988. "Gripen Flies—18 Months Late," 1535.

Jane's Defence Weekly. Jan. 7, 1989. "Taiwan's Ching-Kuo Fighter," 4.

Jane's Defence Weekly. Jan. 21, 1989. "United States Defence Budget: Challenge for President Bush," 86–89.

Jane's Defence Weekly. Jan. 28, 1989. "Soviets Surprise West with New Arms Cuts," 116–17.

Jane's Defence Weekly. Feb. 11, 1989. "Two More Warsaw Pact Nations Cut Arms," 206.

Jane's Defence Weekly. Dec. 16, 1989. "US Army Seeks Euro Partners for ATACMS," 1321.

Jane's Defence Weekly. Jan. 6, 1990. "Into the Next Decade," 18–19.

Jane's Weapon System: 1987–88. Edited by Bernard Blake. 1988. 18th ed. London: Jane's Publishing Co. Ltd.

Johnson, James Turner. 1982. *Just War Tradition and the Restraint of War: A Moral and Historical Inquiry*. Princeton, N.J.: Princeton University Press.

————. 1984. *Can Modern War Be Just?* New Haven and London: Yale University Press.

Karp, Aaron. 1988. "The Trade in Conventional Weapons." In *SIPRI Yearbook 1988: World Armaments and Disarmaments*, 175–201. Oxford: Oxford University Press.

Kavka, Gregory. 1985. "Space War Ethics." *Ethics* 95 (April): 673–91.

Keegan, John, and Richard Holmes. 1986. *Soldiers: A History of Men in Battle.* New York: Viking Penguin.

Kemp, Ian. 1988. "The International Arms Industry: A Final Casualty of the Gulf War." *Jane's Defence Weekly* (July 30): 164–65.

King, Barry B. 1988. "Crisis Facing Israeli Arms Industry." *Jane's Defence Weekly* (Jan. 9): 17–18.

King, Jere Clemens. 1972. *The First World War.* New York: Walter and Co.

Kipnis, Kenneth, and Diana T. Meyers, eds. 1987. *Political Realism and International Morality.* Boulder, Colo.: Westview Press.

Krickus, Richard J. 1986. "On the Morality of Chemical/Biological War." In *War, Morality, and the Military Profession.* 2d ed., edited by Malham M. Wakin, 410–24. Boulder, Colo.: Westview Press.

Lambeth, Benjamin S. 1987. "Theater Forces." In *American Defense Annual: 1987–1988*, edited by Joseph Kruzel, 89–111. Lexington, Mass.: D. C. Heath and Co.

Lao Tzu. 1972. *Tao Te Ching* [excerpts] In *Classics in Chinese Philosophy*, edited by Wade Baskin, 53–87. New York: Philosophical Library.

Lennox, Duncan. 1989. "The Global Proliferation of Ballistic Missiles." *Jane's Defence Weekly* (Dec. 23): 1384–85.

Lok, Joris, 1989. "Dutch Spending Hit by Slow-Down." *Jane's Defence Weekly* (May 6): 786.

Lucas, Hugh. 1988. "Pentagon Corruption: Investigations Could Run After the Election." *Jane's Defence Weekly* (July 2): 1360–61.

Lundin, S. J., J. P. Perry Robinson, and Ralf Trapp. 1988. "Chemical and Biological Warfare Developments in 1987." In *SIPRI Yearbook 1988: World Armaments and Disarmament*, 101–25. Oxford: Oxford University Press.

Mayer, Peter. 1966. *The Pacifist Conscience.* New York: Holt Rinehart and Winston.

Mason, R. A., ed. 1986. *War in the Third Dimension: Essays in Contemporary Air Power.* London: Brassey's Defence Publishers.

McMahan, Jeff. 1989. "Is Nuclear Deterrence Paradoxical." *Ethics* 99 (January): 407–22.

Naess, Arnie. 1986. "Consequences of an Absolute NO to Nuclear War." In *Nuclear Weapons and the Future of Humanity: The Fundamental Questions*, edited by Avner Cohen and Steven Lee, 425–36. Totowa, N.J.: Rowman and Allanheld.

O'Connell, Robert L. 1989. *Of Arms and Men: A History of War, Weapons, and Aggression.* New York and Oxford: Oxford University Press.

Ottaway, David B. 1988. "The Mideast's High-Tech Powder Keg." *International Herald Tribune* (Dec. 20): 1, 6.

Paret, Peter, ed. 1986. *Makers of Modern Strategy from Machiavelli to the Nuclear Age.* Princeton, N.J.: Princeton University Press.

Pollack, Andrew. 1989. "America's Answer to Japan's MITI." *New York Times* (Mar. 5): section 3, pp. 1, 8.

Rapp, G. 1989. "Prototype Crash Adds to Gripen Controversy." *Jane's Defence Weekly* (Feb. 11): 203.

Robinson, Anthony. 1987. "Aerial Warfare." In *The Orbis Military Yearbook, 1987,* 90–99. London: Oriole Publishing.

Ryan, Cheyney C. 1983. "Self-Defense, Pacifism and the Possibility of Killing." *Ethics* 93 (April): 508–24.

Schefter, Jim. 1988. "Missile Killers." *Popular Science* (September): 46–50, 110, 112.

Shang, Yang. 1972. *The Book of Lord Shang* [excerpts] In *Classics in Chinese Philosophy,* edited by Wade Baskin. New York: Philosophical Library.

Sherman, William Tecumseh. 1892. *Memoirs of General W. T. Sherman.* New York: Charles L. Webster and Co.

SIPRI Yearbook 1988: World Armaments and Disarmament. 1988. Oxford: Oxford University Press.

Sivard, Ruth Leger. 1987. *World Military and Social Expenditures: 1987–88.* 12th ed. Washington, D.C.: World Priorities.

———. 1989. *World Military and Social Expenditures: 1989.* 13th ed. Washington, D.C.: World Priorities.

Smith, Hedrick. 1988. *The Power Game: How Washington Works.* New York: Random House.

Soviet Military Power: An Assessment of the Threat—1988. 1988. Washington, D.C.: U.S. Government Printing Office.

Starr, Barbara. 1989. "USA Looks for Safer Nunn Projects." *Jane's Defence Weekly* (Nov. 25): 1147–48.

———. 1990. "A Basis for Control: Ballistic Missile Proliferation." *International Defence Review* (March): 265–67.

Stringer, Hugh. 1986. *Deterring Chemical Warfare: US Policy Options for the 1990s.* Washington, D.C.: Institute for Foreign Policy Analysis, Pergamon/Brassey.

Stubbing, Richard. 1987. "The Defense Budget." In *American Defense Annual: 1987–1988,* edited by Joseph Kruzel, 45–68. Lexington, Mass.: D. C. Heath and Company.

Sundaram, Gown S. 1988. "Peace and the Arms Trade." *International Defense Review* (Sep. 21): 1049.

Sweetman, Bill. 1988a. "B-2: The Shape of Things to Come." *Jane's Defence Weekly* (Nov. 19): 1266.

———. 1988b. "Challenge Thrown Down to Soviet Air Defences." *Jane's Defence Weekly* (Dec. 3): 1377.

———. 1990. "Radical Design of Stealth ACM." *Jane's Defence Weekly* (Mar. 10): 413.

Taylor, A. J. P. 1963/66. *A History of the First World War.* New York: Berkeley Publishing.

Thomas, Ann Van, and A. J. Thomas, Jr. 1970. *Legal Limits on the Use of Chemical and Biological Weapons.* Dallas: Southern Methodist University.

Thurman, William E. 1988. "USAF Defends Stealth Programs." *International Defense Review* 3 (No. 3): 517–18.

Treitschke, Heinrich von. 1963. *Politics.* New York: Harcourt, Brace and World.

Tsipis, Kosta. 1987. "Arms Control Pacts Can Be Verified." *Discover* (April): 79–93.

Wakin, Malham M., ed. 1986. *War, Morality, and the Military Profession.* 2d ed. Boulder, Colo.: Westview Press.

Walzer, Michael. 1977. *Just and Unjust Wars.* New York: Basic Books.

———. 1988. "Emergency Ethics." In *The Joseph A. Reich, Sr. Distinguished Lecture on War, Morality and the Military Profession,* No. 1, given at the United States Air Force Academy on Nov. 21, 1988, pp. 6–21.

Webster's Ninth New Collegiate Dictionary. 1986. Springfield, Mass.: Merriam-Webster.

Westling, Arthur H. 1984. "How Much Damage Can Modern War Create?" In *Future War: Armed Conflict in the Next Decade,* edited by Frank Barnaby, 114–24. London: Michael Joseph Ltd.

Wood, Derek. 1987. "Nunn Initiative Programmes." *Jane's Defence Weekly* (Apr. 11): 644.

Wrixon, Tim. 1986. "C-17: A New Concept." *Jane's Defence Weekly* (Oct. 25): 965–69.

Index